THE
PASTORAL CONSTITUTION
ON THE CHURCH
IN THE MODERN WORLD

De Ecclesia

In Mundo Huius Temporis

THE
PASTORAL CONSTITUTION
ON THE CHURCH
IN THE MODERN WORLD

**Promulgated by Pope Paul VI
December 7, 1965**

Commentary by
GREGORY BAUM, O.S.A.
and
DONALD CAMPION, S.J.

PAULIST PRESS

New York   Paramus, N.J.   Toronto

Nihil Obstat:
Rev. James J. O'Connor
Censor Librorum

Imprimatur:
✠ Leo A. Pursley, D.D.
Bishop of Fort Wayne-South Bend

November 17, 1967

The Nihil Obstat and Imprimatur are official declarations
that a book or pamphlet is free of doctrinal or moral error.
No implication is contained therein that those who have
granted the Nihil Obstat and Imprimatur agree with the con-
tents, opinions or statements expressed.

Library of Congress
Catalog Card Number: 68-16669

Published by Paulist Press
Editorial Office: 1865 Broadway, N.Y., N.Y. 10023
Business Office: 400 Sette Drive, Paramus, N.J. 07652

Printed in the
United States of America
by Our Sunday Visitor Press

Contents

PART I
THE CHURCH AND MAN'S VOCATION

PART II
SOME PROBLEMS OF SPECIAL URGENCY

Commentary

Gregory Baum, O.S.A.

In the *Pastoral Constitution on the Church in the Modern World* the Catholic Church tells men of our age what she thinks of earthly existence, how she regards human life and human work, and how, in cooperation with all men, she wants to solve the many problems that threaten peaceful living and impede the progress that is God's will for the human family.

The Constitution is an extraordinary ecclesiastical document from many points of view. It ushers in a new style of teaching. It takes an approach to human life and history for which there is no parallel in the conciliar documents of the past. It is addressed not only to Christians but to all men of our generation. The document presents the problems of modern life with perception and honesty, and, in the light of the Gospel, proposes some solutions for present difficulties. It does not suggest, however, that the Church has all the answers. "The Church is the guardian of the heritage of the divine Word, from which she draws religious and moral princi-

1

ples, but she does not always have a ready answer to every question" (n. 33).

Wrestling with the social, moral, cultural and religious issues of our age, in union with other men who live in the same human situation, we entertain the Christian hope that the guidance of God will be available to us, and even where we do not see clear solutions at the moment, we trust that more insight will be granted to men who, by being deeply engaged in life, are faithful to their destiny.

A conciliar document is called a "constitution" because it teaches what is constitutive of the Christian faith. The *Constitution on the Church in the Modern World* differs from other conciliar constitutions inasmuch as it does not present Christian wisdom in the form of doctrinal exposition. The document is called a "pastoral" constitution. Pastoral in this connection means that the document presents the realities of our age in the light of the Christian faith. In other words, the Christian faith is taught in this pastoral constitution by proposing an understanding of the present age according to the Gospel and by offering answers to some of the questions raised by the modern world according to the same Gospel.

I
PREFACE

The Preface of the Constitution clarifies what is meant by "the world" (n. 2). It is well known that in the Johannine writings of the New Testament "the world" usually stands for the human family inasmuch as it is wounded and deformed by sin. "Do not love the world, or the things that are in the world. If anyone loves the world, the love of the

Father is not in him; because all that is in the world is the lust of the flesh, and the lust of the eyes, and the pride of life" (1 Jn. 2, 15-16). This Johannine terminology has often been adopted in sermons and catechisms and in the spiritual literature of the Christian Church. In the ordinary Christian vocabulary "the world" used to mean the ungodly world, the seat of selfishness and pride. There is, however, another way of using the same term "the world". We may call "the world" humanity wounded by sin and yet redeemed by Jesus Christ, or the world of man and his environment, created and redeemed by the Father in and through his Word. According to this understanding the world is good. Despite its sinfulness, the human family has been restored to the friendship of the Father through Jesus in the power of the Spirit. In the Constitution, the world stands for that "world which, in the Christian vision, has been created and is sustained by the love of its creator" (n. 2).

One of the great difficulties in writing the Constitution was to find a language and a method of presentation that would be understood by Christians and other men alike. The conciliar discussion revealed that the bishops had various views on the matter. There were some who suggested that the Church should address herself to the world on the basis of natural wisdom and natural law. This, they believed, was the common ground between Church and world, and only after the natural order had been thus treated should the Constitution add the message of the Gospel which determines the Christian existence. Other bishops felt that the Church of Christ may address the world on no other basis than the Christian Gospel. The Church, they thought, should tell the world the content of the divine message we believe, and if men are touched by the power of God's Word, they will find faith and join us in the family of the faithful.

The conciliar commission that drafted the Constitution followed neither of these approaches, though they retained the special concerns of both groups of bishops. The commission tried an altogether new approach. After analyzing the present world, the commission set down how the Church, in the light of revelation, understands the vocation of man on this earth, how we can build a community of brothers, and what is the meaning of man's work in this world. The Constitution expresses Christian wisdom, but it attempts to do this not in specifically Christian language but in ordinary words of everyday experience. It wishes to withdraw neither into the specialized terminology of Christian dogma nor into the abstractions of a particular philosophy. The Constitution attempts to describe in concrete terms what human life means to the Christian, how he intends to build community with other men, and how he regards human activity here on earth. This approach is based on the hope that men everywhere, listening to our understanding of human existence and the creation of human solidarity will understand what we want to say and, in fact, may find that this understanding of the human situation does not differ much from their own. The Constitution is based on the hope that there is a common ground between Church and world, a ground that is not definable simply in terms of natural truth and natural values, but, rather, in terms of the actual historical experience of human life and human community.

What is the basis for this hope? It is a doctrine, taught in the *Constitution on the Church*, according to which the God of mercy is at work not only in the Church but, in fact, in the whole of humanity, calling man into communion with one another and with himself. Human life as it exists in history includes the divine call which, freely and without merit, comes to men wherever they are. This is the basis for the hope that people who live deeply and who reach out for the meaning of life will understand the Church's description of man's existence, redeemed and transformed by Jesus.

Since the doctrinal basis of this approach is so important, we must analyze the teaching of the *Constitution on the Church*. The question is asked (n. 2) whether God had been redemptively at work among men before the time of Jesus and beyond the house of Israel? Was there salvation outside of the biblical people? The question is crucial. Are we to think that the Lord of mercy remained inaccessible for the 500,000 years that mankind has existed on this earth? The *Constitution on the Church* assures us that God has never left himself without a witness. From the beginning of human existence, God promised salvation and initiated the dispensation of mercy that was to find full expression in the Church of Christ. The conciliar text teaches that God's merciful action among the nations *prefigured* the Church, that his work in Israel *prepared* the Church, and that his mercy, wrought in Christ, is fully *manifested* in the Church. The call of grace went out to men from the beginning. Following an expression derived from the Fathers of the Church, the Constitution speaks of the Church from the time of Abel. From the beginning the mercy of God acting among men was a foreshadowing of the Church. From the beginning God intervened on behalf of the many. Stories such as that of Noah's ark reveal the plan of God to offer salvation not only to individuals but to a community. We realize that grace, wherever it is granted, creates friendship

or communion among men, and in this way pre-
figures the Church.

The *Constitution on the Church* asks another
question (n. 16): Is the God of mercy at work, in
this age, only in the Church or is he at work in all
of humanity? The answer reiterates the teaching of
God's universal will to save, found in n. 2. We are
told that wherever men reach out for the true and
the good, be this in other religions or in any human endeavor, God himself is at work in them,
moving them toward salvation. This merciful presence of God among men, gratuitous and unmerited
as it is, is always granted in view of the Church of
Jesus Christ. Through his grace in humanity God
prepares the full manifestation of his mercy in the
covenanted community of believers. God's universal call to grace is therefore both preparation for
and anticipation of the coming of Jesus Christ. This
was the meaning of grace in the situation of Abra-
ham, this it was in the situation of Israel, and this
it is in the situation of the human family today.

The *Constitution on the Church* (n. 16) applies this teaching to all men in a radical way. We
are told specifically that the man who does not
acknowledge God is not thereby necessarily deprived of God's transforming mercy: "Divine providence [does not] deny the helps necessary for
salvation to those who, without blame on their part,
have not yet arrived at an explicit knowledge of
God and with his grace strive to live a good life."
We must take care not to misunderstand this teaching to mean that man can save himself by his own
virtue and goodwill. Every man is in need of the
gratuitous gift of divine mercy to advance on the
way of salvation. The teaching of the *Constitution
on the Church* is that wherever men reach out for
what is true and good, for building communion

rather than destroying it, for dying to selfishness and gaining a new freedom to love others, God's mercy is at work in them. The Church "knows that this is given by him who enlightens all men so that they may finally have life".

This teaching is endorsed and expanded in the *Constitution on the Church in the Modern World.* The Christian faith proclaims two truths that are not easily reconciled: we believe that Christ is the one mediator between God and man, and at the same time we hold that God is redemptively at work among all men. The *Constitution on the Church* shed light on this mystery by insisting that the grace of God outside of the Church is always granted in view of Christ and his body. The *Constitution on the Church in the Modern World* goes a little further. It presents the Christian as the man who has become the brother of Jesus by faith, and who, through the power of the Spirit, is being transformed in the likeness of Jesus and thus as son has access to the Father. It is the believer's share in the paschal mystery, Christ's death and resurrection, which constantly draws him into greater likeness with Christ and makes him more truly son of the Father. "The Christian," we read, "is certainly bound both by need and by duty to struggle with evil through many afflictions and to suffer death, but as one who has been made a partner in the paschal mystery, and as one who has been configured to the death of Christ, he will go forward, strengthened by hope, to the resurrection" (n. 22). The Constitution then continues, explicitly and clearly: "This sharing in Christ's resurrection holds true not only for Christians but also for all men of good will in whose hearts grace is active invisibly. For, since Christ died for all, and since all men are in fact called to one and the same divine destiny, we must hold that the Holy Spirit offers to all the possibility of being made partners in the paschal mystery in a way known only to God."

This, then, is the doctrinal foundation of the Church's approach to the world of men. It undoubtedly represents a most significant dogmatic development. In the teaching of Vatican Council II, the Catholic Church not only changes her manner of approaching other people on practical issues, but also modifies her vision of faith regarding who other people are and what God is doing in their midst. Founded upon this teaching, the Church is deeply convinced that a description of human life according to the Gospel, even while avoiding the language of dogma, will be understood by other men and appreciated by them as describing the same basic mystery which they experience in their own existence.

II
INTRODUCTION

As God taught the people of Israel through events taking place in their history, so he continues to teach the Christian people. The Church must listen to the voice of God coming to her in the present situation. The conciliar text speaks of the "signs of the times" to which the Church must always pay attention. The expression "signs of the times" occurred many times in a previous draft of the Constitution, but since the scriptural meaning of this expression refers, rather, to the signs preceding the second coming, the final text uses this expression very rarely. The conciliar text prefers to speak of the signs of God's presence in history.

We must listen to the situation in which we

live. What, then, must the Church discover about the world in which she lives? In the first place she must understand the present generation and the contemporary age in order to grasp the questions that men are asking and to understand their dreams and ideals. Since Jesus has come to be the answer of God to the human situation in need of deliverance, the Church must find out what issues preoccupy men today. The Church must know the questions of men before she is able to formulate any answers. If she does not first listen, she is not really talking to anyone.

The Church must listen to the present situation not only to discover the questions that are being asked; she must also listen to discover the replies which God is now giving to these questions in history. What are the forces of healing and reconciliation at work in the world? Where is God building his kingdom? Often the Church must participate in the fears and conflicts of mankind not to offer her own solutions but, rather, to join herself to the work God is now doing among men. The signs of God's presence and work in the world are manifold. We must dare to listen to them even when they spell out God's judgment on the Church. Thus the contemporary quest for authenticity and honesty and, on a social level, the search for justice and peace are works of God in the world, works which, at times, reproach the Church for not having sought the same values as eagerly or for not having sought them with others. The Church must listen to the world before she can speak to it. This is a new doctrinal principle in the Church's understanding of redemption.

The *Pastoral Constitution on the Church in the Modern World* tries to present a realistic picture of the modern world. It acknowledges that modern life has really changed. The strongest kind of language is used here. The conciliar text speaks of social, cultural, moral and religious transformations that have taken place. It speaks of a broad and deep revolution that is coming to pass in humanity. This courageous acknowledgement of a new situation is contrary to a widespread ecclesiastical tendency to belittle the changes in life. Again and again we have been told that life has always been as it is now, that young people have always felt that the generation of their parents did not understand them, that there is really nothing radically new in our situation and that, therefore, the answers given to man's problems in the past will suffice for the present. Such an understanding of the present reassured the ecclesiastical organization that it could continue to apply the formulas of the past, and if people would not listen, then this was their own fault. Measured by this ecclesiastical tendency, the Introduction is a startling piece of work, a powerful statement of where we stand, a realistic analysis of the present situation of the human family.

From the beginning, the Introduction stands watch over the following chapters of the Constitution. When it asserts that in the modern world "mankind substitues a dynamic and more evolutionary concept of nature for a static one" (n. 5), it offers a criterion by which the entire Constitution will have to let itself be evaluated.

At the same time, there is nothing utopian about the evolution that is being described. The vision is biblical, and the human situation is revealed in its ambiguity. The modern world shows itself as "at once powerful and weak, capable of doing what is noble and what is base, disposed to freedom and slavery, progress and decline, brotherhood and hatred". Both are there, the good and the evil; every step toward human progress giving promise of greater well-being may still be abused by man's malice to produce greater destruction. However much man moves toward a better society, the need for redemption does not become less, for the more glorious the possibility of helping men and removing their misery, the more powerful also become the means by which man may destroy himself. This is not said in disparagement of social progress. On the contrary, the conciliar text shows the need to reach out for a progress that humanizes and spiritualizes earthly life, and at the same time reveals that this progress is never definitive, remains threatened, and hence is in constant need of redemption. Even the unification of man in a single family of brothers remains, on this earth, vulnerable to becoming a means for a more universal revolt against God.

For this reason the Church derives her hope from a principle beyond this world, from Jesus Christ, who is the same, yesterday, today and forever. The self-revelation of God in Christ gives the Church deep convictions about the meaning of life and inspires her with the hope that these will make sense to the people with whom she engages in conversation. The ambiguity of existence experienced today in such unprecedented sharpness gives rise to an almost universal self-questioning. Who are we as man? How can we, who are alone, become friends? What is the meaning of our effort here on earth? Is it a waste of time? Is there a way out of our alienation? Because of Christ, the Church believes that she has answers to these questions, answers that are at once new and old. When we are open to the wisdom of the Gospel, we often feel that somewhere in us, at some deep level, we have known it all from the beginning.

III

THE DIGNITY OF THE HUMAN PERSON

Chapter I of the Constitution presents many elements of what may be called a Christian anthropology. Who are we? The Church intends to tell the world what we think about man. As we mentioned earlier, we do this with the deep conviction that because the destiny of all men is one and the same —namely, communion with God and with one another—the basic experience of being human is very much the same among Christians and other people. Besides, there is a special reason why we want to tell the world what we think of man. Many ordinary people, both uneducated and learned, entertain certain strange ideas about how Christianity pictures man, and they totally reject this picture.

Many uneducated people whose contact with the Church has been superficial believe that Christians think man becomes a sinner through his involvement in earthly things. In their opinion, Christians regard the attachment to earthly things as evil, and hence it is by despising visible things that they reach out for the heavenly ones. Because what counts for them is the reward of eternal life, they do not engage in the great quest of transforming the world of the present. They are willing to suffer all kinds of hardships, trusting that at the end they will rise with Jesus Christ. For this reason, these people believe that Christians despise the good, happy and joyful things of this world and thus are the enemies of life.

Even some learned men whose contact with the Church has been superficial entertain certain strange ideas about how the Church envisions man. These men believe that Christians regard man as composed of two parts, body and spirit, a composition in which the bodily part is the heavy, sluggish principle pulling man down into the slavery of the flesh, and the spiritual part, the soul, is the light principle, superior to the body, elevating man to the values that really count. According to them, the greatest ideal of the Christian is to become less and less determined by the bodily principle and more and more by the spiritual one. The Christian seeks to be delivered from the body for an untrammeled life of the spirit. Virginity, withdrawal, contemplation, patience in suffering, accepting the world as a cross—such things supposedly comprise the perfect Christian ideal, the highest life; and while not all Christians are able to reach out for this high life of the soul, they greatly long for it, and hence look down upon the worldly things in which they must regretfully be involved.

To appreciate Chapter I of the Constitution, we must keep in mind that one of its purposes is to refute the ideas which some people (perhaps even Christians) have of the Christian view of man. The conciliar text defines man in scriptural terms as created in the image and likeness of God. How is this imaginative language explained? Man is the image of God because he is able to respond to him. Man can listen, choose and reply. He is responsible. He is a person. It is suggested, moreover, that calling man the image of God the creator means—and there is scriptural evidence for this—that man, too, in his own way, is creator. Man is the master of the things of the world and is destined to transform the earth and human life. From the same scriptural account, telling us that man is created in the image of God as male and female, we learn that man is a social being. Man is not alone. It belongs to his very essence to be related to others. It is through communion between persons—the conciliar text uses this term—that man is constituted as a person.

This characterization of man, while derived from Scripture, is in harmony with our experience. We are responsible; we are workers; we are in community. In our involvement in life we constantly use our bodily and spiritual faculties, and yet we are one. The conciliar text emphasizes the unity of man. We acknowledge our bodily activity, and appreciate our body as the instrument through which we are inserted into history; at the same time we are also aware of a level of life so personal and intimate that bodily activity does not describe it adequately. "By his power to know himself in the depths of his being he rises above the whole universe of mere objects" (n. 14). Man discovers himself as belonging to a spiritual order. It is significant that the text avoids the technical terminology of antiquity: instead of presenting a definition of the soul, the text simply describes how man becomes aware of the interior reality of his life, a reality that transcends the bodily dimension. The reference to his soul as "spiritual and immortal" (n. 14) was added to the conciliar text in a later draft on the suggestion of a Council father who felt that the anthropology of the chapter was moving too far away from traditional teaching. The expression was thus inserted, but its meaning is not derived from a particular Scholastic teaching; rather, it sums up the characteristics of man described in the preceding sentences.

It is in and through his mind that man transcends his own bodily existence and the material world in general. At the same time, this mind does not isolate him but, rather, brings him into touch with other men and the depth of reality. The conciliar text affirms man's vocation to knowledge and understanding.

A special section deals with man's conscience

(n. 16). According to a narrow Scholastic tradition, conscience is an act of the practical intellect by which a man judges what is to be done in the concrete circumstances of life. According to a more universal Christian tradition, conscience is understood as the core of a man's inner life where he is in dialogue with God. Conscience is the sacred source of morality in human life. The conciliar text emphatically endorses this tradition. "Conscience is man's most secret core, and his sanctuary. There he is alone with God whose voice echoes in his depths. In a wonderful manner, conscience reveals that law which is fulfilled in the love of God and one's neighbor. Through fidelity to conscience Christians are joined to other men in the search for truth . . . . " (n. 16). This teaching clarifies what is meant by the biblical expression that man is created in the image and likeness of God. Man is able to respond to God; he is responsible to God; he is responsible for his life.

This teaching, moreover, shows that we cannot understand the deepest dimension of man without taking into account the invisible God. A man listening to his conscience is not locked into the sphere of his own wisdom; he is open to the transcendental; he is in touch with the invisible immanent. According to the teaching of the conciliar document, therefore, the fidelity of man to his conscience is what traditional theology has called the supernatural. It belongs to the order of grace, of revelation, of redemption. For this reason, the Constitution can say that "through fidelity to conscience Christians are joined to other men in the search for truth". This teaching demands that we have the greatest respect for any man who has based his life on a moral choice. Such a man has entered into the dialogue of salvation with God.

The consciences of people sometimes lead them to erroneous positions, as the conciliar text admits. But at the same time the man who follows his conscience is open to reality, and hence the very fidelity to an erroneous conscience is a way of discovering the error and bringing the moral judgment into greater conformity with reality. It is through fidelity to a living, sensitive and searching conscience that men are led to an objective morality.

Man is called to responsible and free life according to a law which is best summarized in terms of love of God and love of neighbor. It follows, therefore, that moral conflicts arise in human life, but these do not result from the division between body and soul or from the disparity between this life and the life to come. According to Scripture, as the conciliar text assures us, the basic moral conflict in man's heart, which is the source of all other clashes in human life, is the result of sin. Man has refused to obey the redemptive will of God, his Father. Experience confirms that we are born into a state where self-centeredness and self-aggrandizement are natural to us and militate against the call to love and humility that we hear in our conscience. This connatural selfishness is all-pervading. "Man . . . is divided in himself. As a result, the whole life of men, both individual and social, shows itself to be a dramatic struggle between good and evil, between light and darkness" (n. 13).

The world of man is mysterious. "Both the high calling and the deep misery which men experience find their ultimate explanation in the light of divine revelation (n. 13). It is for this reason that the final section of Chapter I openly declares that the mystery of man is totally disclosed only in the incarnate Son of God, the man Jesus Christ, who suffered, died and rose for us. In Jesus it is revealed to us who God is; in Jesus we also are shown who man is and what is his destiny. In his innocent death on the cross, Jesus reveals to us the radical hostility of sin to life; in his perfect surrender to the Father during his life and beyond into resurrection, he reveals to us the destiny of every man. Christ is the way for every man to become truly himself. By entering into Christ's dying, we are increasingly delivered from the power of sin; by entering into his resurrection, we are freed for a new life of love, a life that will reveal its total dimension only in the age to come when all men shall comprise the household of God.

The conciliar text, as we have mentioned, indicates that the paschal mystery is present and active everywhere in humanity. In some fashion, the Son of God by his incarnation has united himself with every single human being. Christ is the key to the riddle of human existence.

The christological understanding of man makes the phenomenon of atheism particularly difficult to understand. Since the root of human dignity lies in man's call to communion with God and since he is invited to this conversation with God from the very circumstances of his origin, it is difficult to understand how men can be atheistic or, more precisely, how men can survive as human beings when they repudiate the living God. Yet the modern world is full of atheists, some of whom are even linked to us in friendship. It is therefore in this first chapter that the Constitution dedicates several paragraphs to the problem of atheism (nn. 19-21).

Two opposing tendencies were represented at Vatican Council II. Some bishops desired a new condemnation of atheism, especially of dialectical materialism, the official philosophy of communism and the basis for the anti-religious activity of the

Communist States. Other bishops, however, believed that another condemnation of atheistic materialism by the Church would not achieve any positive effect. It could even be regarded as an undue interference in the political sphere, and hence such a gesture could be dangerous in areas where the co-existence between men who believe in God and men who do not is of crucial importance. These bishops thought that Christians should face the atheistic convictions of their fellowmen with openness, engage in study and dialogue with them, and in this way discover what is the divine mission of the Church to men formed in an atheistic culture. After a debate carried on in the conciliar hall (and outside of it), the policy followed in the conciliar text was determined by the bishops who were against a new condemnation of atheistic materialism. The Constitution declares that the Church always has and always will repudiate any system of thought and action that denies the existence of God and his loving concern for mankind. At the same time the Constitution demands that Christians make an effort to understand the various forms of atheism which exist in our midst, that they engage in sincere and prudent dialogue with atheists and that they collaborate with them in the endeavors to better man's life in the earthly city.

What is the usefulness of dialogue with atheists? At first sight it might appear that such conversation must by necessity turn into a disputation about the existence of God and his concern for the world. However, the Constitution suggests that men are atheists for many reasons, and that it is important for Christians to discover precisely what these reasons are. Atheism is not a spontaneous movement, we are told, or a universal movement found in all periods of history, but, rather, a movement of protest or critical reaction against religious belief. Thus, atheism often has philosophical and social roots. In some cases at least, the atheist rejects an image of God that, because of his own misunderstanding or, perhaps, the false ideas suggested by his Christian environment, is just a figment of the imagination, so that by repudiating this image he is not rejecting the true and living God. Some men have rejected God in a gesture of protest against evil in the world. The Constitution leaves open the possibility that there are declared atheists who have not said "no" to the living God in their hearts and that what ultimately counts in them is their attitude to human life and the world in which God manifests himself.

Since atheism is a movement of reaction, the responsibility of the Church in its genesis may be considerable. These matters will have to be examined in dialogue. The Constitution insists that we must examine together with atheists how we understand the world in which we live and what is the meaning of our action in it. Today the Catholic Church insists that the firm belief in the age to come does not make Christians indifferent to social and political change; on the contrary, such a belief impels them to engage themselves more deeply in transforming the earthly city. The victory of Christ in resurrection is, for the Christian, not totally in the future; he anticipates it and lives from its power when he wrestles with forces of darkness in this world and serves with others to establish a human society in which dignity, peace and justice are more clearly expressed. Dialogue with atheists, especially with atheistic Communists, will have to establish whether the opposition of Marxists to religion is based on the inner logic of their philosophical system or whether it is simply a reaction against the social effects of religion as the founders of Marxism understood them in the last century. It is conceivable that atheistic Communists, while remaining faithful to the Marxist interpretation of reality, could abandon their opposition to religion if they saw that the spiritual outlook of religion does not inspire indifference to the miseries on earth, but, rather, a firm determination to engage in social action to relieve injustice and exploitation.

Since the Constitution echoes the orientation of Pope John's *Pacem in terris,* we shall cite a highly significant passage from this encyclical:

> It must be borne in mind, furthermore, that neither can false philosophical teachings regarding the nature, origin and destiny of the universe and of man be identified with historical movements that have economic, social, cultural or political ends, not even when these movements have originated from those teachings and have drawn and still draw inspiration therefrom. For these teachings, once they are drawn up and defined, remain always the same, while the movements, working on historical situations in constant evolution, cannot but be influenced by these latter and cannot avoid, therefore, being subject to changes, even of a profound nature. Besides, who can deny that those movements, insofar as they conform to the dictates of right reason and are interpreters of the lawful aspirations of the human person, contain elements that are positive and deserving of approval?
>
> It can happen, then, that a drawing nearer together or a meeting for the attainment of some practical end, which was formerly deemed inopportune or unproductive, might now or in the future be considered opportune and useful (nn. 159-160).

IV
THE COMMUNITY OF MANKIND

The second chapter is intimately related to the first. If man is understood as the image of God, then this determines him as one who is in conversation with God and as a creator in the world, and, more than that, as one whose nature is to be related to others. This was the anthropology proposed in Chapter I. The biblical account "Male and female he created them" (Gen. 1, 27) suggests that the social dependence or interrelatedness of man is not an element added to his existence as a human being but is an essential dimension of what it means to be a person. It is this dimension that is brought out in Chapter II.

In the present age we have become more deeply aware of the interrelatedness of human life. This is true on a large scale where the problems that face humanity can only be solved by a growing interdependence and collaboration; this is also true on the level of personal life where we have become more aware that our relationship to others largely determines who we are. This is the overwhelming experience of men of our times. This is, moreover, the clear teaching of Scripture. "Christian revelation contributes greatly to the establishment of this fellowship and at the same time promotes deeper understanding of the laws of social living with which the creator has endowed man's spiritual and moral nature" (n. 23). By bringing out the social dimension in the Christian understanding of man, the Gospel becomes a relevant force in the reconciliation of men in our age.

Mankind on this earth forms a single family. This is the basic message of Scripture. They have a common origin and a common destiny. The insep-

arable nature of the twofold commandment to love
God, and after him the neighbor, reveals that no
man can seek to do the will of God without joining
others in creating a community of love. Faithful to
his vocation, man must be concerned about the
common good of the society to which he belongs,
even unto the common good of the whole human
family. Through increasing interrelatedness and
coordination of efforts, he must be more deeply engaged in promoting the common good and removing the burdens on the human community. We
have here a restatement of the principle of socialization which we find in the encyclicals of Pope
John XXIII. The Constitution finds a deeper
theological context for this teaching in the very
nature of man as the image of God.

The creation of the vast network of interrelations which characterizes modern society bears
with it certain dangers. Every organization can be
used for evil and exploitation. Large organizations
may suppress individual persons, or smaller groups
within it, in the free exercise of their prerogatives.
The conciliar document here reiterates, in a theological context, the principle of subsidiarity which
is the necessary complement, and sometimes the
corrective, of the principle of socialization. According to the principle of subsidiarity a larger society
may not take over the functions of smaller societies
living within it when these latter are able to fulfill
their proper functions adequately. Social progress
therefore remains ambiguous and must constantly
be watched. In addition, the social organizations of
men must always be improved. In order to achieve
this, what is required is education of the people and
social systems that permit increasing participation
of the many in the making of public policy. "Praise
is due to those nations where it is possible for the

largest possible number of citizens to take part in public affairs in a climate of genuine freedom. . . . " (n. 31). We note, in passing, that the same principles apply to the societal life of the Catholic Church. If we hesitate too long in applying these principles in the Church herself, there is a real danger that the world may not believe our sincerity in proposing these principles in a conciliar document.

The teaching of the Pastoral Constitution is far removed from an old-fashioned individualism. Human society is not the product of many who, of their own free will, came together to form a society. Man is, by nature, social. Conversely, it is precisely the social nature of man, his dependence on and his concern for others, that makes him truly a person. "The social nature of man shows that there is an interdependence between personal betterment and the improvement of society" (n. 25). The aim of society is to promote the person. "Life in society is not something accessory to man himself; through his dealings with others, through mutual service and through fraternal dialogue, man develops all his talents and becomes able to rise to his destiny" (n. 25).

This teaching affirms the understanding of man in contemporary personalist thought; it invalidates the individualism which lingers in so much of religious thought. Christian life is not the quest for personal salvation. Vatican Council II rejects any ethic of withdrawal, whether it is based on religious, political or moral concepts. There is an indissoluble connection between the growth of the human person and the advance of the society in which he lives; for this reason every human being, by living intensely, is in a dialectical situation where he is constantly drawn beyond himself to be concerned about others and, at the same time, led to deeper self-discovery through his communion with others. On another level, this same dialectic appears in society where the emphasis on the dignity of the human person and on the rights and freedom belonging to man is accompanied by the realization that these rights and this freedom can be assured for all members of society only if they are promoted and protected through a growing web of interrelations and social structures of increasing complexity.

Chapter II supplements the christological understanding of man drawn in Chapter I. That God has created man in his own image also brings out the unity of the human family and the social dimension of his personal existence. Man is dependent upon his fellowman. The mystery of life in Father, Son and Spirit is reflected, however weakly, in the unity of human family. "If man is the only creature on earth that God has wanted for its own sake, man can only fully discover his true self in a sincere giving of himself" (n. 24).

The idea that the person is defined by his relation to others is traditional in the theology of the Trinity, but the application of this idea to the theology of man is rather new. We look back to a long tradition of teaching, according to which man was defined in himself, in terms of his human nature, intellect, will and the other parts of his mental and physical constitution. In this tradition it was only after we had grasped the essence of man that we turned to his relationships to others to study how they perfected him or how they affected society. The Constitution seems to follow contemporary personalist thought when it regards man's relationship to others as part of his essential personal structure.

This shift in the understanding of the human

person will have wide consequences in various fields. The most obvious one is that of morality. The Constitution refers to this briefly (n. 30) when it insists that "a merely individualistic morality" will no longer suffice in our age. "The best way to fulfill one's obligations of justice and love is to contribute to the common good according to one's abilities and the needs of others, even to the point of fostering and helping public and private institutions devoted to bettering the conditions of life." The area of moral responsibility has enormously increased. Many aspects of life about which Christians in the past were able to shrug their shoulders with good conscience have, through the changes in society, entered into the field of their moral concern. We are just beginning to learn what this means for the ideal of Christian holiness.

In connection with this deeper understanding of man as being essentially in relation to others, it would have been proper to indicate the need for renewing the whole of moral theology in the Catholic Church. That this did not happen, either in this chapter or in any other conciliar document, is one of the great lacunas of the Council. Some bishops speaking in the conciliar hall made references to this, speaking of the biblical teaching on law and Gospel, the problem of legalism, the relation of morality to the historical situation, the renewal of family morality, etc. The conciliar document does not face these issues systematically. The deeper understanding of the interrelatedness of the human person would have enabled the Council to move beyond the legalism fostered in the Church whenever there was no clear distinction between the obligations created by ecclesiastical legislation and the demands of the Gospel of Jesus. This deeper understanding of the human person would have

enabled the Council to transcend the old tradition
in moral theology in which the norms of human behavior were sought in universal laws rationally derived from a human nature impersonally conceived.
The Council could have initiated an approach to
moral theology on the basis of the essential human
interrelatedness, the value of the human person
and man's dialectical relationship to a community
of others. This did not happen. Some of the foundations for this renewal, however, are found in
Chapter II.

V
Man's Activity in the Universe

Chapter III interprets the meaning of human
work and man's effort in transforming society and
creating history. The chapter is intended as a dialogue with the world. It was composed with full
awareness of the misunderstandings which others—
men of the world, whether Marxists or not—have of
traditional Christianity. People often think that
the Christian hope for the age of glory leads to a
neglect of temporal values; they claim that the
Christian religion lessens independence in the human culture it seeks to pervade or even produces an
estrangement of man from himself; finally, they
suspect that Christian doctrine is intrinsically opposed to free research into the secrets of nature and
the actual events of history.

What is the Christian understanding of work?
From the beginning of time men have labored to
better the circumstances of their lives. From the
Christian viewpoint this human activity is in ac-
cordance with the will of God. Man created in
God's image was made a worker or creator in the

universe, and by his efforts through the centuries, both as an individual and in community, he has unfolded the work of the creator. Spurred on by grace and led by the Spirit, he has contributed to "the fulfillment in history of the divine plan" (n. 34). Looking upon the world and contemplating the meaning of human activity, the Christian is "convinced that the achievements of the human race are a sign of God's greatness and the fulfillment of his ineffable design" (n. 34). The man of faith who understands his vocation as a human being will not be tempted to neglect the temporal society; rather, he will be totally dedicated to transforming it according to the will of God.

At the same time this realization of the divine plan in history must not be understood as an ultimate goal apart from, and beyond, the transformation and salvation of persons. Human activity takes its significance, its measure and its value from the human person (n. 35). The progress of human civilization, of arts and science, of the integrated society, are values only inasmuch as they serve the human person. Their goodness lies in the extent to which they transform men, making them more profound, more generous and more responsible.

The Christian, then, acknowledges the autonomy of the created order, the life of man and society. He believes it is God's will that the laws and values inherent in human life must be discovered by man, put to use and regulated by him, and that he is, indeed, autonomous in this endeavor. There can be no conflict from the wisdom derived from honest research and the truth of the Christian faith since both derive from the same God. The Constitution makes an oblique reference to the past, lamenting the blindness of Christians who have not respected the independence of science and have thus provoked men to suspect that there is in Christianity a hidden opposition between science and faith. The footnote refers here to a recent biography of Galileo. This is an all too modest allusion to an ancient tradition of fear in the Church—the fear that man's free research might result in a discovery opposed to divine revelation or, at least, to the doctrinal and organizational structure produced by the Church.

At the same time this positive understanding of work and the progress of human civilization must not blind us to the ambiguity of human life. The Constitution insists that progress can be a source of temptation (n. 37). Human selfishness is at all times capable of abusing man's greatest achievements by making himself, or his own group, the center of life. Human life always implies a wrestling with the powers of destruction. However much man advances in self-possession and the integration of society, he remains in need of redemption. The call of the Gospel that we shall "not be conformed to this world" recalls the threatened situation of human life and culture; rather, it is directed against conversions can men use the values of this life, not for self-aggrandizement, but in the service of brotherhood.

The vulnerable situation of human civilization gives particular meaning to the Gospel. The message of Christ lays bare the illness of society and makes man face the powers of destruction inherent in his life in order that from the acknowledgement of the darkness in him he may more readily follow the Spirit into the freedom to love and to serve. The strong denunciation of the world which is proper to Christian prophecy is not directed against human life and culture; rather, it is directed against the illness of human society and hence, despite its harshness, is in favor of growth, health, development and expansion.

At the end of Chapter III the christological viewpoint is made even more clear. By the death and resurrection of the man Jesus Christ, we are assured that the reconciliation of the human family as a single brotherhood is possible. In fact, Jesus is both the accuser and the reconciler, working in the history of man through the paschal mystery. The chapter here repeats the doctrinal position which forms the basis of the entire Pastoral Constitution: "Constituted Lord by his resurrection and possessing all authority in heaven and on earth, Christ is now at work in the hearts of men by the power of his Spirit; not only does he arouse in them a desire for the world to come, but he animates, purifies and strengthens the generous aspirations of mankind to make life more humane and to conquer the earth for this purpose" (n. 38). The humanization of man and society is the work of Jesus in the power of the Spirit.

On this doctrinal basis, the chapter is able to make its final interpretation of Christian eschatology. All Christians believe that the new age will come upon us as a judgment, and that man, reborn in God's grace, shall find beatitude in that new age. But prior to the Council Christians differed greatly in estimating human life here on the earth, human work and culture, and the progress of society. Are all these elements which are under divine judgment, and hence destined to disappear, or are they in some way touched by human redemption and hence preserved for an existence in the age to come? Must the Christian love the earth with caution and suspicion since its value is only provisional, or may he love it without reserve as embodying a reality that is to be saved for eternity?

Without deciding in favor of any school of theology or any particular thinker, the Constitution gives a positive interpretation of earthly existence. Thanks to the action of Christ in the world and his creation of charity in the human heart as the driving force of transformation, "the body of a new human family grows, foreshadowing in some way the age which is to come" (n. 39). The new age, in other words, is in some way anticipated in the victory of love here and now. Jesus Christ and the new humanity are already invading our lives. He is already with us, though it is also true that he is always coming, as judge and redeemer, detecting our illness and healing our wounded body.

Is this positive eschatology, which enables the Christian to embrace the created world with the confidence that redemption is already at work in it, an endorsement of the theological position of Teilhard de Chardin? I do not think so. The text has been carefully composed. In Scripture the texts employing cosmic imagery are open to two interpretations: they may refer either to the redemption of the cosmos or simply to the redemption of the human family and the earthly elements serving this redemption. The same openness is preserved in the Constitution: "Charity and its works will remain, and all of creation, which God made for man, will be set free from its bondage to decay" (n. 39). Catholics are free to suppose that divine redemption is cosmic; they are also free to suppose, if they so prefer, that the Gospel of Christ simply deals with the redemption of man. All Christians are bound, however, to appreciate this earthly city as the place where the victory of Christ over sin is present in many ways, a victory serving the kingdom of God and to be established in glory at the end of time.

VI
THE ROLE OF THE CHURCH
IN THE MODERN WORLD

Chapter IV deals with a subject that has become extremely difficult at this particular moment in the Church's history. What is the mission of the Church in the world? At one time, we thought that this was a comparatively easy question to answer. The Church was sent, as were the apostles, to announce Jesus Christ to the world of men and make disciples of all nations. The mission of the Church was to make Jesus known where he was not accepted and to make him more deeply loved and obeyed where he had been received.

A number of theological trends have made this understanding of the Church's mission rather incomplete and hence somewhat inadequate. What are some of these trends? In the first place, we have become more aware of the merciful action of God in the whole world, and hence we are firmly convinced that the Spirit is present in human life prior to the preaching of the Gospel. Second, we appreciate more than ever before the solidarity of the Church with the entire human family, and we acknowledge our common responsibility in overcoming division in human life and establishing the conditions of peace among men. Third, we have a deeper conviction that the redemption which Jesus has brought initiates a true transformation of human life so that to be more Christian or more open to the Spirit means also to be more human. Fourth, we have discovered that in the salvation history which God has appointed for his Church, it is often through the world—i.e., through people outside the Church—that we have been taught, corrected and thus assisted in the pursuit of greater fidelity to the Gospel of Christ.

The problem of determining the precise mission of the Church in the human family has become very difficult, and Vatican Council II did not attempt to give a definitive answer to this. In the *Decree on the Church's Missionary Activity,* the obligation of the Church to obey the command of Christ to preach the Gospel to all nations is spelled out. The *Declaration on the Relation of the Church to Non-Christian Religions* lays the doctrinal foundation for the Church's dialogue with followers of other religions and encourages cooperation between religious bodies in matters of common human and spiritual concern. Let us admit that it is not easy to bring together these two documents in perfect harmony. The *Constitution on the Church in the Modern World* adopts still another viewpoint in regard to the Church's mission. It tries to lay the foundation for the Church's dialogue with humanity and the "proper fostering of mutual exchange and assistance" in common concerns in order to translate the demands of human solidarity into historical reality. However, because of the difficulties in relating this mission of the Church to her total mission, many questions are left quite open.

Chapter IV outlines what the Church is able to offer to the world through her understanding of man and her insistence on the dignity of the human person (n. 41), through her efforts to strengthen the bonds of human community and overcome the powers of division and enmity (n. 42), and, finally, through the deeper meaning and importance she gives to human activity and daily work (n. 43). Chapters I, II and III are here reviewed from the viewpoint of the contribution they make to the human family in which the Church lives and to which she inseparably belongs.

The Church serves the world by announcing and promoting human values. To be Christian means to be fully human and to be engaged in building a community of love. At the same time, this action of the Church is not a purely this-worldly affair. In its exercise the Church lives from the Gospel. Because of the Gospel the Church is particularly sensitive to the forces that undo human dignity and human community, and it is therefore her task and service to the world to reveal the illness of society. The Church's mission, even in regard to values of this world, is prophetic (n. 41). She denounces the inherent dangers threatening the movements that promote human freedom and the brotherhood of nations. Her prophecy, however harsh it may sound, is not directed against the world of men. Its intention is therapeutic, laying bare the illness from which we suffer to prepare the way for health and recovery.

When the Constitution speaks of "the Church", what is meant is not so much the institutional Church as the Christian people. It is specifically pointed out that "the Catholic Church holds in high esteem what other Christian Churches and ecclesial communities have contributed and are contributing cooperatively to the realization of this aim" (n. 40)—namely, offering help in making the human family and its history more human. The Church, then, in the sense of the Christian people, belongs to the human family, declares herself in solidarity with it, offers her help and, in fact, also receives help.

The Church is being helped by the world! The Constitution openly avows this (n. 44). The believing community has always used the culture of its generation to express the Christian faith. The political concepts of society have had their impact on the social organization of the Church. "It is the task of the whole People of God, particularly of its pastors and theologians, to listen to and distinguish the many voices of our times and to interpret them in the light of the divine Word" (n. 44). We must be open to the assistance of human wisdom in the pursuit of the proper task of the Church in making relevant the Gospel of Christ and spreading the redeeming power of the Christian message.

The world of men helps the Church in another way, as the Constitution suggests when it speaks of the failings of the Church: "The Church is not blind to the discrepancy between the message she proclaims and the human weakness of those to whom the Gospel has been entrusted" (n. 43). We are told that we must be conscious of our failings, reflect on them and take them seriously. The Church must become more and more mature in her responses to human and divine realities, and the path to this goal is clearly laid out: "The Church also realizes how greatly she needs the maturing influence of centuries of past experience in order to work out her relationship to the world" (n. 43). It is at least suggested here that in her relationship to the world the Church is made aware of her own illnesses and that the judgment of God also comes to her through the experience of humanity and the consciences of other people. Therefore, it is hardly too much to assert that the Church needs the world of men in order to be, become or remain the People of God faithful to the Gospel of life. Through isolation the Church harms the world and harms herself.

The solidarity of the Church with humanity is therefore a dynamic one, a living relationship; thus, the difficulty of expressing the Church's mission in the world in a simple formula should not surprise us. In the total plan of redemption which God has for the human family, it may even be true that in different centuries the Church has understood or will understand her mission to the world in somewhat different ways. However, there is no danger of confusion here, since the Church always remains the listening Church—listening to the Spirit speaking in the Gospel and the hearts of men.

The *Pastoral Constitution on the Church in the Modern World* affirms, as no ecclesiastical document has done before, the historical character of human existence. Man is an historical being. His situation in history modifies his self-understanding, and he himself may be said to change. This is true in regard to his personal and his communal existence. The Church herself is in history. Her own self-understanding is subject to growth and deepening. The Church differs from the family of men in which she lives and to which she belongs by virtue of the mysterious presence of Christ. This presence is so deeply inscribed in her life that no human infidelity can ever undo the union of the Lord and his people.

Commentary

Donald Campion, S.J.

I
THE DIGNITY OF MARRIAGE AND THE FAMILY

Traces of the complicated legislative history of the *Pastoral Constitution on the Church in the Modern World* remain enshrined in the text as it was finally approved and promulgated on December 7, 1965. The complexity of the issues involved and the relative newness of topics discussed in the document's pages had made it seem unlikely at times that Vatican Council II would ever be able to produce a meaningful statement in this field.

One editorial decision that eventually made the task possible called for a division of the proposed Constitution into two parts. The first, already examined in the previous commentary, would be presented as primarily *doctrinal* in its concern; the second, treating of "some problems of special urgency", would seek principally to answer *pastoral* needs. It would be a mistake, however, to suppose that matters of doctrinal importance are in fact confined only to the first part, or that any section of the entire text departed from that fundamental pastoral orientation prescribed for the Council by John XXIII and repeatedly ratified by the manifest will of a great majority of the conciliar fathers.

It is interesting to recall that when a preliminary draft of the *Constitution on the Church in the Modern World* as such was first drafted in the early winter of 1963, the heavy stress was on doctrinal issues, and these were discussed primarily in a technical fashion. As a matter of fact, this initial draft never won full clearance from the Council's coordinating commission. In the late summer of the same year, however, a new effort was made to draft a text. This document, chiefly the work of a group brought together by Cardinal Suenens, spoke along new and more pastoral theological lines. Both texts, of course, embraced a far broader scope than that to be found in the drafts *On The Social Order* and *On The Community of Nations* proposed by the preparatory theological commission prior to October 1962.

None of the provisional texts mentioned thus far ever received clearance for general distribution among the Council fathers. A breakthrough came with the creation of a special drafting commission of eight bishops at the close of Vatican Council II's second session. This group met with a small band of *periti* at Zurich in the early part of 1964. The text they produced was the one actually debated in the *aula* or Council hall in October 1964.

Of particular interest to us is the fact that the new commission also composed a set of appendices or *annexa* that were eventually distributed to the Council fathers, though they were not to be the immediate subject of debate in the Council.

After the conciliar debate, the commission was expanded to provide a broader spectrum of views

and charged with revising the text one more time.
A decision was then made to incorporate into the
documents the substance of the *annexa* as far as
possible. Here was the point of insertion for much
of what would become Part II of the Pastoral Constitution as we finally received it from the Council.

Though this revision was largely completed in
the period from December 1964 to February 1965,
the document itself would undergo one further and
final editing in November 1965 when the Council
had discussed some items once more and the fathers had cast their *modi* or suggestions for last-
minute corrections or emendations of the text. Of
some significance is the fact that in the very last
stages of the editing of the text as we know it, the
greatest controversy and widest division of opinion
among the Council fathers still centered chiefly on
certain sections of Part II, "Some Problems of Special Urgency".

It should not surprise us that there was division
of opinion or judgment in the Council even at so
late a date. On practically every issue that came
before it, Vatican Council II divided into two or
more camps. Moreover, the Pastoral Constitution
by its very nature, and Part II in particular, called
for new confrontations and the inevitable uncertainties that accompany them. Paul VI has aptly
described the mood of the Church in undertaking
this task. In an address on December 7, 1965, at the
ceremony in which the final voting and promulgation of the Council's remaining documents took
place, he said:

Never before perhaps . . . has the Church felt the
need to know, to draw near to, to understand, to
penetrate, serve and evangelize the society in which
she lives, and to come to grips with it, almost to run
after it, in its rapid and continuous change. This at-

titude, a response to the distances and divisions we
have witnessed over recent centuries, in the last century and in our own especially, between the Church
and secular society—this attitude has been strongly at
work in the Council.

Part II of the Pastoral Constitution, we are told
in an introductory article (n. 46), will consider
"some problems of special urgency affecting the human race at the present time". It is important to
note the tone and spirit in which the Council proposes to take up these matters. It aims to make this
consideration "in the light of the Gospel and of
human experience". More significantly, the Council does not propose to give answers as such, but
rather to shed light by which to search for answers
to questions of such complexity. We know from the
drafting commission itself that the most vexing issues, specifically insofar as clashes of judgment
within the Council were concerned, had to do with
the morality of modern war, aspects of marriage
and family morality, and the phenomenon of atheism. Certainly, opinion in the Council at times split
sharply on these topics. It is necessary to recall this
fact in interpreting or assessing evidences of compromise in the formulation of certain key statements as they appear in the definitive text.

Chapter I of Part II seeks to foster the dignity
of marriage and the family. Though it reveals
clearly the continuity over the centuries of certain
major elements in the Christian understanding of
marriage, no reader can mistake the text's parallel
concern to advance and deepen this understanding,
particularly through a remarkable stress on the
pivotal role of conjugal love.

Indeed, this emphasis seemed so strong to some
that they found the proposed chapter theologically
immature, equivocal and regrettably silent on cer-

tain essential points. In particular, these critics insisted on a flat affirmation that procreation is the primary end of marriage; lacking that, they demanded the deletion of the whole chapter on the score that the principal questions at stake were to be handled by the recently created papal commission on population, marriage and family morality. The text survived, however, and stands now as an authoritative statement of Christian teaching.

As a matter of fact, the chapter opens with a reminder of the link between sound family life and the well-being of individuals and society (n. 47). The Council proposes to address itself to evils such as polygamy, "the plague of divorce", selfishness and "illicit contraceptive practices" that it views as a threat to marriage and the family. It also takes note of problems affecting marriage and the family that emerge from contemporary economic systems, from cultural trends and from the phenomenon of modern population growth. By presenting some key points of Catholic teaching in a clearer light, it seeks to offer men guidance in upholding the institutions of marriage and the family.

Perhaps no other element in the Christian understanding of marriage receives stronger emphasis in the Constitution than its *interpersonal* character. "The intimate partnership [of married life] established by the creator. . . is rooted in the conjugal covenant of irrevocable personal consent" (n. 48). By careful choice the Council speaks here not of a contract but of a covenant. To arrive at a knowledge of the relationship between spouses, we must look to biblical imagery and what it tells us of God's relation to his people. Here is the model of love and fidelity on which true married love and life must be patterned.

The drafting commission repeatedly refused to

make explicit reference to the conventional distinction between primary and secondary ends of marriage. In one instance, it coupled its refusal to accept a proposed emendation in that direction with a reminder that the papal encyclical *Casti connubii* itself used variations in speaking of ends of matrimony. Throughout this section, in defense of its way of treating the question, the commission stressed its pastoral concern. Perhaps the commission's care in this matter appears most clearly in its statement immediately after speaking of children as the "supreme gift of marriage" (n. 50). In going on to speak of the practice of "true conjugal love" as having the aim of cooperating with the creator, it makes clear that in doing so it does not intend "to underestimate the other ends of marriage" (n. 50). A similar indication of the commission's mind appears in a note in which it refused to say that conjugal love, independently of any procreative intention, does not justify the conjugal act. Another emphasis in the same section (n. 50) that is worthy of note is on the responsibility of parents with respect to a decision concerning new parenthood. Although the commission modified the text on this matter to the extent that it dropped out a reference explicitly excluding others from participation in the final judgment here, its own wording remains sufficiently clear when it states that "the married couple themselves . . . must ultimately make these judgments before God" (n. 50).

With respect to this and similar judgments concerning parenthood and other elements of marital morality, the Council by no means underplays the significance of objective standards or norms in the formation of such judgments. Thus, in n. 51, the Constitution states clearly that judgments in these matters cannot depend solely on "the good inten-

tion and the evaluation of motives". At the same
time, the commission charged with drafting this
text was not content to derive these "objective criteria" from mere biologism. Such standards must
rest on a comprehensive consideration of the demands of the total human person. N. 51, it should
be noted, contains one of the most widely known
footnotes (118) of any conciliar document. It was
included at the explicit request of Pope Paul himself. Whatever the Pope's intentions may have been
in proposing this footnote or whatever the understanding of the commission or of all the Council
fathers in accepting it as part of the text, it seems
generally agreed now that the note of itself, with
its references to papal pronouncements on birth
control prior to Vatican Council II, did not reverse
the trend of the Council's teaching in the body of
the text, nor did it alter the state of debate on the
matter that had existed since Pope Paul's own an-
nouncement on June 23, 1964 of his creation of a
commission to study questions in dispute about
marriage and birth control.[1]

Chapter I on "The Dignity of Marriage and
the Family" closes with a strongly pastoral note
(n. 52). This section speaks of the meaning of fam-

---

[1] For a fuller understanding of the controversy that sur-
rounded the entry of footnote 118 into this text of the
Council, it may be profitable to consult several articles: Fr.
Gregory Baum, O.S.A., "Birth Control—What Happened,"
in *Commonweal* (December 24, 1965); John T. Noonan,
Jr., "Contraception and the Council," in *Commonweal*
(March 11, 1966); John L. Thomas, S.J., "What Did the
Council Say on Contraception?" in *America* (February 26,
1966); John C. Ford, S.J., "More on the Council and Contraception," in *America* (April 16, 1966). There is also an
interesting account, written at a later date and with more
background information, in Xavier Rynne's *The Fourth
Session* (Farrar, Straus and Giroux, 1966).

ily life for the different members of a family and of
the important roles played by all. At the same time
the text calls attention to the responsibilities to be
shared by different individuals and social institutions such as the State. All have a stake in the welfare and health of the human family. The Council
is never content to offer merely pious exhortations,
but calls attention to the need to consult the med-
ical, biological, social and psychological sciences in
seeking to preserve sound marriage and family life.
Proper support is also demanded for associations—
here one thinks of groups such as the Christian
Family Movement and various types of Cana programs that have flourished in the United States—
that will introduce younger people to a sound view
of marriage and the family or that will foster a
steady and healthy growth in family life already be-
gun.

II
THE PROPER DEVELOPMENT OF CULTURE

The *Pastoral Constitution on the Church in the
Modern World* next takes up the extremely difficult topic of culture and its proper development.
The difficulty here lies partly in the novelty of the
questions involved. The Council fathers rightly
point to the ambiguities or uncertainties present
even in the scientific disciplines of sociology, anthropology and history concerning culture and its
meaning. Thus, when the Constitution poses a definition of culture in an introductory article (n. 53),
it actually offers something more in the way of a description than of a technical definition. It is perhaps
on this account that some bishops, in their criticisms of the text before the final vote, complained

that the style was verbose and journalistic rather than the technical and tight style of a conciliar text in the traditional sense.

Perhaps the key aspect of culture set forth in this introductory definition is its living, historical quality. Here the Council fathers have stressed the sociological and ethnological understanding of culture. It is certainly of interest to note that in describing the scope of culture the Constitution explicitly includes religious practices. This should serve to settle the dispute still heard in some quarters as to whether or not religion, in the sense of religious practices and institutions, can be a proper subject for study by the social scientist. Clearly the Council fathers thought the answer was "yes". In locating culture in history, the Council also recognized that there can and would be a plurality of cultures in human experience. At the same time, the Constitution goes on to speak of the evolution in our day of a "more universal form of human culture" (n. 54) as a result of contemporary developments.

In fact, the Council's judgment is that man stands in a "new age in human history" (n. 54). What are the marks of this new age and culture? One is the sharpening of man's critical judgment. Another is the understanding arrived at through a more profound exploration of human activity carried on with the aid of psychological studies. A third is a sense of history with an accompanying emphasis on the fact of change and evolution. Still another mark or characteristic is that of the spread of new forms of culture and the emergence of what the Council fathers speak of as "mass cultures".

It may be of interest to note that the document in this section (n. 54) refers to the impact of industrialization. We know from the official records that the drafting commission refused to introduce a discussion of automation at this point despite a request to this effect by some Council fathers. In a later section of the Constitution (n. 66) reference would be made to automation, but only in a passing way. Vatican Council II made no attempt to enter into a discussion of the many aspects of this modern phenomenon or of its profound social, economic and political implications.

Along with the rise of culture must be seen the growth of a widening sense of participation among many men and women of our times. Behind this sense of participation lies an awareness of independence as well as of responsibility for developments in all spheres of life. At this point in the discussion the Constitution refers to "the birth of a new humanism" (n. 55). One can readily and properly see here a forecast of the encyclical of Paul VI, *Progressio populorum (On The Development of Peoples)*. From the official records we know that the drafting commission of the Pastoral Constitution explicitly recognized that the key idea here was one of a growing consciousness among men of their responsibility and the significance this has for the maturity of the human race. There is also a noteworthy shift from an emphasis on building a new world to one of building a "better world" (n. 55). This will not be a world free of problems and troubling conflicts, however. Many of these are now taken up by the Pastoral Constitution. Wisely the Council fathers preferred to raise here a series of questions rather than to attempt oversimplified solutions. Although some critics would complain in advance that the technique of posing questions was one more proper to a classroom than to an ecumenical Council, the final decision was to take a stand for an approach that would encourage dialogue and avoid dogmatism in such complex areas. While the Council gives all proper credit to the preservation of traditional cultural values, it allows also for the necessity of developments in human life, understanding and education that will more fully respond to the enormous advances in science and technology. The text even refuses to propose a solution on the thorny question of the legitimate autonomy of human culture that is to be more than "purely earthbound" (n. 56).

To the extent that the Council deals with the relations between faith and culture, it takes a very positive and open stance. The Christian, essentially a pilgrim, must keep an awareness of "the things that are above" (n. 57). Still, God's work here on earth is truly our own. In its discussion of progress in contemporary science and particularly in the development of scientific method, the Constitution betrays little of the nervousness that characterized much religious thinking in the age of the unhappy war between science and religion. The Council fathers are fully aware of the problems posed by a spirit of "scientism" but they refuse to ignore the positive values of modern science as such. In concluding a discussion on this topic, the text even speaks of "preparation for the acceptance of the message of the Gospel" (n. 57), an echo of the ancient conception of creation as a *preparatio evangelica*.

It is important to note the confidence with which the Council speaks of God revealing himself through the culture proper to each age. One can find here a wealth of meaning with respect to a similar acceptance by the Church of the true significance of literary genres and historical forms of written teaching for a proper understanding of God's revelation throughout the ages. In its discussion of the links between the Gospel and culture, the Pastoral Constitution also makes one somewhat cryptic reference to a relation between liturgical forms and man's spirit of liberty or freedom. We know again from the official records that the drafting commission itself had in mind a reference here to Eastern liturgical traditions.

The latter half of this chapter takes up a series of important requirements for the proper development and enjoyment of human culture. One concerns the freedom of culture from undue influence by alien forces. Here the Council makes clear its view that culture can never be subverted to ideological ends. "The scope of public authority does not extend to determining the proper nature or forms of human culture" (n. 59). Equally important is the insistence of the Pastoral Constitution on the freedom of those who would engage in the development of culture and their right to information. Here at the outset the Council is speaking of a general right. At a later point (n. 62) it will apply this principle directly to those engaged in theological inquiry.

The liberating aspect of contemporary culture is also stressed. The Council fathers gladly welcome the opportunity offered mankind to free men from "the curse of ignorance" (n. 60). This opportunity must be seized and care taken to see that the benefit of education for full responsibility and participation is extended to all: the rural population, workers and, specifically, women. In connection with the last point—that is, the rights of women— the document is more explicit and unqualified than some desired. Here again, according to the official record, the drafting commission explicitly refused to accept a recommendation to alter the last sentence of n. 60: "Everyone should acknowledge and foster the proper and necessary participation of women in cultural life." The commission refused to add any qualification about women's proper role being restricted to home and family. This statement is fully in accord with the recognition accorded women in contemporary world society by John XXIII in his encyclical *Pacem in terris*.

The Council recognizes the difficulties to be overcome in bringing about this spread of culture among all groups in modern society. One of the greatest problems for those trained in a classical tradition of knowledge and culture is the problem of a lack of synthesis of all knowledge and arts. The day of the "universal man" (n. 61) is at an end. How then is there to be a true integration of knowledge rather than a splintering? Perhaps a key here, though it is not developed by the Council at this point, is to be found in the concept of socialization and its suggestion of the possibility of team effort replacing the solitary universal thinker. The Pastoral Constitution in fact calls attention to the help to be had from modern techniques in the circulation of books. It is probable that the Council fathers were not thinking explicitly of the highly advanced methods of retrieval proposed for libraries of the future, but it is clear that they see great possibilities for overcoming the difficulties that would limit universal sharing in the fruits of modern culture.

In a concluding section of this chapter on culture (n. 62), the theme of the relation between culture and theology or Christian teaching is explored. The Constitution has no hesitation in praising the usefulness to theology of new methods of scientific investigation and literary criticism. It likewise sees great value for pastoral theology in the developments of modern psychology and sociology. The arts and literature contribute greatly to the life of the Church, and the text insists that artists must be made to realize this. The Church stands ready and eager to make use of what the arts have to offer, even in the sacred moment of liturgical worship.

A major emphasis in this concluding section (n. 62) is on the necessity of dispelling any false dichotomies or conflicts between religion and secular knowledge. The Christian is a man of his time. Ecclesiastical sciences and the other sciences must be in continuous dialogue, which is by definition dialogue in both directions. In speaking of the contact between the seminary and the university, for instance, the Council makes it clear that the benefits will not be simply for the secular academician or merely for the seminary student. There is a serious requirement that the ecclesiastical scholar himself benefit from contact and intellectual exchange with prominent men of learning in other disciplines.

All of this, of course, would be meaningless if true freedom for scholarly pursuits were not guaranteed to all who are committed to engage in them. In its *Decree on Priestly Training,* Vatican Council II had already affirmed a spirit of open inquiry and research as a valuable and necessary element in the structure of a contemporary seminary or university. In a closing paragraph, it takes up still more explicitly the necessary guarantee of freedom to the ecclesiastical scholar. One general criticism that had been made of the chapter as a whole, as recorded in the comments submitted before a final vote was taken in the Council, was that the text of this entire chapter failed to take sufficient note of abuses committed in the name of culture. Throughout, the drafting commission refused to sound a pessimistic or negative note. This was notably true in its procedure with respect to proposed changes in the concluding sentences of the chapter. For the sake of sound scholarship in the sacred sciences, the Pastoral Constitution insisted that "the faithful, both clerical and lay, should be accorded a lawful freedom of inquiry, of thought and of expression, tempered by humility and courage in whatever branch of study they have specialized" (n. 62). Despite the suggestion of some who may have seen here the "Teilhardian optimism" that they discerned elsewhere in the chapter, the drafting commission refused to drop the sentence as a whole. It likewise refused another suggestion that it eliminate the clarifying phrase "both clerical and lay". In rejecting this suggested emendation, the drafting commission noted that the text should stand, "for those words are in response to a suggestion made in the Council hall". It is widely reported that the original suggestion for specifying that this was a right of both clerics and laymen came from the then newly-appointed archbishop of Turin, Francesco Pellegrino. Commentators were quick to note that the new archbishop had himself been for many years a university professor of history.

The commission's way of dealing with one final suggested change in this sentence perhaps best reveals the spirit of the entire chapter—in fact, of the entire Pastoral Constitution and, one might even add, of Vatican Council II itself. Some Council fathers suggested that the word "courage" be dropped from the text of the final sentence. In rejecting this proposed change, the interesting comment of the drafting commission was: "That the text should stand for courage is not useless." Certainly the fathers of the Council themselves had had firsthand experience of the truth of this dictum. It might also be added that this dictum certainly would have won the hearty assent of John XXIII.

III
ECONOMIC AND SOCIAL LIFE

Of the five chapters in the second half of the *Pastoral Constitution on the Church in the Modern World*, the chapter on problems arising in connection with man's socio-economic life sets forth the least novel teaching. The Council fathers themselves note that principles of justice and equity have been worked out, and that in modern times, especially, the Church has enlarged upon them (n. 63). For this reason the text speaks of a wish "to reiterate these principles in accordance with the situation of the world today" (n. 63) rather than to develop untouched areas.

What this text refers to is, of course, the body of teaching from the encyclicals of Leo XIII down to the pronouncements of John XXIII in *Mater et Magistra* and his last testament *Pacem in terris*. Despite the fact that the Council is professedly drawing on a well-established body of papal teaching for the major lines of this chapter, it is not without interest to note that some of the fathers objected, before the final vote, to what they felt was a spirit of demagoguery in some places in the text. Such critics objected, for example, to the fact that there was in their view too much stress on the rights of workers and not enough on their duties. Others felt that the very title of the chapter, "Economic and Social Life", suggested a Marxist flavor. As an overall judgment of the chapter, it is safe to say that the general lines remained open and progressive despite the reservations expressed by some.

The chapter opens with a flat statement of the close link between man's economic life and his human dignity. Equally flat is the finding that there are errors on all sides in contemporary debates between economic theories and systems. What the Council wishes to stress is the added factor in today's world scene of a growing conviction on the part of all men that economic and social inequalities can and must be removed. Men feel today that there is a new possibility of doing something about age-old evils. There must be changes in men's ideas and attitudes, but there must also be changes in the socio-economic order and structures.

In insisting that the economy must be made to serve mankind, the Pastoral Constitution makes its own the phrase "growing human aspirations" (n. 64). Productivity must be put at the service of man and for the Council this means every man.

The stress on growing human aspirations is a fitting prelude to an expression of concern about the need to promote economic and social development everywhere. One hears in this section (n. 64) a prelude to Paul VI's *Progressio populorum*.

In lending support to the need for economic development, however, the Constitution is quick to add the need for human control through participation at all levels, even the international, in guiding this development to truly human goals. The document condemns with equal vigor individualism pursued in the name of freedom and collectivism pursued in the name of efficiency or science. At the same time, it emphasizes the duty of all citizens to contribute to the national effort to restore or build up the economy (n. 65). Although the text does not identify any groups by name, its criticism of those who fail to carry out their responsibilities as citizens by refusing to put land to good purposes for production or by refusing to invest their wealth in the national economy is quite evident. The acute problems posed for many Latin American economies by the lack of responsibility of wealthy and landed people is a matter of record.

Throughout this chapter and that on the political life of the community, the Council fathers tend to skirt the issue of the right to revolution. However, in speaking of the special problem created for the world today by the enormous imbalances between groups of rich and poor, farmers and city dwellers, etc., the text does mention the need for vigorous action to right the wrongs resulting from such imbalances. The Constitution clearly states the need to guarantee occupational and territorial mobility to all groups. At the same time, it calls attention to the care that should be provided for special groups such as migrant workers (n. 66).

Since the Constitution has called attention elsewhere to the modern phenomenon of leisure, it does not spend much time on this aspect of man's economic life today. Emphasis is given to the value of labor as a human activity by noting that man can never be viewed as a mere instrument. The greatness of work is that man finds his personality in it, and for the believer there is the added realization that it is the means by which man shares in God's work of creation and Christ's redemptive labor (n. 67).

One section of this chapter would be read with great interest by those familiar with the writings of Leo XIII, Pius XI and Pius XII—that concerning concepts of economic participation and conflict. The Council fathers had already indicated that the heightened sense of a right to participate in meaningful decisions extended to all areas of life. Here they emphasize the application of this principle to the economic arena. The Council fathers took pains to emphasize the active character of the participation to be enjoyed by workers in the framing of broad economic decisions. They had noted explicitly that the formation of unions and collective bargaining are among the fundamental human rights. When one or more of the bishops questioned the use of the phrase "fundamental rights" (n. 65), the drafting commission insisted that "fundamental" be kept, since, as they noted, this is the terminology common to practically all constitutional legal systems today. Similarly, the text emphasizes the need for *active* participation by the people involved (n. 65). For those who recall the language of Vatican Council II's *Constitution on the Sacred Liturgy,* the Latin expression "actuosa participatio" will be familiar here. The expression conveys the same meaning, and in a sense the fundamental reasoning is identical in both instances.

Although there were some who wished to qualify or limit much more drastically the affirmation of the right of workers to strike, the text as it reads is very clear and forthright on this point. In a sense, the implication is that any civil law of a State should conform to the rights of the citizenry rather than that the rights of the citizenry should be tailored to conform to civil laws. Finally, it might be noted that the Council preferred to refrain from a more explicit statement about the types of organizations which workers might join. There was an explicit request by a number of the Council fathers for a clear reference in the text to the famous vocational or industrial groups or classes made popular by Pius XI in his encyclical *Quadragesimo anno.* The drafting commission, in refusing to introduce the proposed emendation concerning this reference, simply noted that the sort of organizations or structures envisioned by Pope Pius XI were not excluded in this context.

The paragraphs on the common purpose or destiny of all created things aroused considerable debate among the Council fathers. The text insists in n. 69 that goods are always "common" property, even when they are the lawful possessions of an individual. The wording that was finally approved seemed to many to be too strong in emphasizing the communitarian aspect of property. But the drafting commission, with the eventual vote of approval of the vast majority of the fathers, held firmly to the need for underlining the most ancient Christian tradition on this point. It is true, however, that it became necessary to add a number of citations from the Fathers as well as a quote from a radio message of John XXIII to reassure those who found the text too disturbing as it stood. The major conclusion flowing from this stand finally taken by the Council is that obligations in the area of the distribution of created goods are fundamental obligations in both charity and justice. Justice, it should be noted, will in some instances demand that men sacrifice more than what is superfluous of their own possessions in order to meet the needs of their neighbors.

An equally controversial point concerned the question of the man in extreme necessity who has a right to take from the riches of others what he himself needs. The Council fathers plainly affirmed this right, but out of regard for those who raised the specter of fostering "revolution", they agreed that the reference here should be to the single individual's right, thus avoiding any suggestion of promoting the concept of conspiracies. However, there is no doubt about the stress that the Council places on the rights of the needy in extreme circumstances.

Another interesting emphasis in the conciliar text concerns the approval given to various communitarian or collective ownership structures in places where these have long been in force. Here the Council was obviously responding to criticisms raised during the early stages of preparation of the Pastoral Constitution by bishops from Africa and some parts of Asia and Latin America. Their common complaint about earlier drafts on this topic was that the statement of rights too closely identified Western structures with those demanded by some natural order of things. At the same time the Council recognizes that in some societies new economic structures such as a social or welfare system should be welcomed as a sound development in the direction of securing the common purpose of all goods (n. 69).

With respect to the distribution of goods and money in the world economy, the Pastoral Constitution is content to call attention to certain objectives that must be kept in mind when decisions are being made by individuals, groups or the public authority. It is clear that broad decisions affecting economic policy in a country or group of countries can work hardships or injustices on individuals within those countries or in other parts of the world. This is particularly true with regard to underdeveloped countries and regions. At the same time the Council fathers were careful to allow for the fact that some radical measures such as deflation may be necessary at times. If such a policy as a deflationary one should be necessary, however, those responsible for the adoption of the policy must have regard for the impact it may have on certain groups within the country itself or in others which are dependent upon the national economy (n. 70).

The statements in the Pastoral Constitution that

concern ownership of property follow fairly closely those contained in papal pronouncements over the past seventy years. It is interesting to note that a key argument in the presentation of a defense of the concept of private ownership turns on the link between private property and personal freedom. The Council speaks of private property as "one of the prerequisites of civil liberties" (n. 71). This sort of argumentation was developed particularly by John XXIII in *Mater et Magistra*. However, the text of the Pastoral Constitution does recognize the diversity of forms of private ownership. It is also clearly stated in the text that there is no contradiction between affirming the right of private ownership and the actual fact of public ownership in given instances. Finally, whatever the right of private ownership in itself, it is clear from the statements of the Council fathers that there can be urgent need for reforms to secure the fair distribution of income. These can and sometimes will include even extensive land reforms, although the Constitution insists on some fair recompense.

The chapter on socio-economic life concludes fittingly with high words of praise for Christians who involve themselves in direct social action (n. 72). There can be no question about the appropriateness of such activity for the Christian, since it is here seen as a logical consequence of his total Christian commitment.

IV
THE POLITICAL COMMUNITY

After its discussion of man and his relation to the economic community, the Pastoral Constitution takes up the question of modern political life and its impact on the human persons who make up the political community. There were some bishops who approached this topic with considerable concern. They would have preferred to reduce the entire fourth chapter of Part II of the Pastoral Constitution to a statement of a few basic principles of political philosophy. In some instances they raised a doubt as to whether or not civil authorities would resent a conciliar pronouncement on the score that it was a usurpation of the authority of the State. The drafting commission made it clear that its comments on the modern political scene were to be taken as a phenomonological description of the times. Moreover, the drafting commission, with the eventual approval of a great majority of the Council fathers, chose to confine itself to a description of the contemporary cultural, economic and social evolution of many peoples today rather than to choose the less dramatic term of "progress". Though the term "transformations" (n. 73) raised anxieties in the minds of some because of a suspected overtone of materialism, the general thinking of the Council was that the developments we see around the world today are best described in that way.

In the opening section of this chapter (n. 73), the Council looks at the profound political changes that have made themselves felt in the lives of most peoples. Behind these changes the fathers saw an awareness of human dignity that led to a concern for the rights of all men. Closely linked with this is the desire for *active* participation that had already been discussed in relation to man's role in the economic order. In reporting in a positive fashion what it saw in the contemporary political scene, the Council singles out for mention the tendency of peoples to reject governments that impede civil or religious freedoms. For its part, the Council notes that some present-day governments could be so classified. It makes no specific mention of the governments it has in mind; rather, it is content to merely indicate a general support for the concept of limited government. If its discussion of modern political trends sounded overoptimistic to some of the fathers, the majority were willing to support the description given in the opening section of this chapter.

The Pastoral Constitution conceives of the community as a multi-faceted entity. It is one in which all contribute in some way to the common good. However, one characteristic is necessary for it to be classified as a free political community: the right to choose the form of government and the method of selecting leaders is to be left to the free will of the citizens. The official records of discussion on the last draft of the Pastoral Constitution make it clear that the Council wanted to formally express this concept of the importance of freedom with regard to the range of government. In the same section the Council fathers assert the right of citizens to defend themselves against abuses when they "are under the oppression of a public authority which oversteps its competence" (n. 74). Here there is a concern to keep any such resistance within the greatest possible limitations, limitations that seem to be suggestive of the conditions necessary for a just war.

One other point in n. 74 worthy of special note is the Council's reference to a "dynamically conceived common good". There is here a clear reference to the concept of the common good developed by Pope John XXIII in *Pacem in terris*. Some Council fathers feared that this use of the term "dynamically conceived" would be dangerous in that it might convey to some an "evolutionary" sense or provide a line of defense to the Communists. But since the phrase remained in the final text, one can only conclude that the Council as a whole felt this qualification of the traditional concept of the "common good" was necessary in our day.

The Pastoral Constitution goes on to speak of what might be considered as an ideal political structure. After beginning this discussion with the broad rubric of a demand for the widest possible political participation by all citizens, it then praises a defined constitutional system and suggests a division of roles and powers of public authority along the lines set forth by Pope John XXIII in *Pacem in terris*. It notes particularly that the government must respect those lesser groups who may have little chance to make their voices heard. In an interesting passage the Council fathers note the significance of "socialization" (n. 75) as a modern phenomenon that is characteristic of our age. After mentioning this factor of modern life, it proceeds to note the importance of political participation as a countervailing force in the presence of this growing tendency toward interdependence of men in society.

In listing some cautions with respect to political life, the Pastoral Constitution notes particularly the danger in a protracted suspension of constitutional rights or process and warns against a tendency toward excessive nationalism. Politics, the fathers remark, is an honorable profession for the Christian (n. 75) and it is up to the Christian in the political community to behave as a model of respect for liberty and diversity of views and of a willingness to labor for the common good. It is perhaps also interesting to note that throughout this discussion of the political community and the political process, the conciliar document makes no reference to a Christian or Catholic political party as either a desideratum or a necessity.

The closing section of this chapter on political life deals with the touchy topic of the Church and politics. It is stated that in a pluralistically organized society it is especially important to clarify the relation between the Church and the world or general society. The Pastoral Constitution touches the heart of the matter when it speaks of the Church in relation to society as being "the sign and safeguard of the transcendental dimension of the human person" (n. 76). It is this function above all that distinguishes the Church from the political society insofar as the two are in any way comparable.

In another way, the Council fathers tried to mark off the Church and to make distinct her role with respect to the political community. The flat assertion is made that the question of means is important here. The Church, by definition, is committed to use the means that are appropriate to her as revealed in the light of the Gospel. This question of appropriateness of means or of acceptable ways by which the Church may participate in some sense in political affairs is also dependent on an evolving concept of the general welfare. It would be wrong to conclude that the Church is here trying to spell out minimum terms for co-existence with some enemy force. What the Council seeks is to make clear what the Church considers to be her proper function in regard to political affairs in our time.

Even when she is situated in an atmosphere of political oppression, the Church nevertheless claims the right not merely to function in some narrowly religious sense—i.e., the conducting of devotional exercises—but also to teach her doctrine and to make pronouncements in the name of that social teaching. However, at the same time the document makes it clear that whatever intervention the Church may make must be one made on the proper terms and according to appropriate means. If she does not remain true to herself, the Church can scarcely render any worthwhile service to the political common good.

V
MAINTENANCE OF PEACE AND ESTABLISHMENT OF A COMMUNITY OF NATIONS

As was said above, the two most troublesome issues that confronted the Council fathers in the drafting of the *Pastoral Constitution on the Church in the Modern World* were birth control and family morality and the question of war and peace in our time. The last chapter of Part II of the Pastoral Constitution deals with the question of peace and mankind's task of bringing into existence a community of nations.

At the outset of this last chapter, our attention is turned to the human family in a time of supreme crisis in its advance toward maturity. The document speaks with a tone of high emotion and almost of anguish. It calls attention to the close harmony between the Gospel message and the loftiest hopes and aspirations of the human race. It notes that these aspirations face their greatest obstacle in the form of the threat of universal war. Thus there can be no turning aside from the vocation of Christians to be "advocates of peace" (n. 77).

To anyone familiar with the impassioned words

of Paul VI at the United Nations in October 1965, the style and substance of the passages of this chapter dealing with the nature of peace and the horror of war will be familiar. One also hears echoes, again and again, of John XXIII's *Pacem in terris*. Peace is not a mere absence of war (n. 78). Rather, peace is the true fruit of love and justice. Above all, the bishops wish to make completely clear the vocation of every Christian to be an artisan of peace. They have words of praise for those who choose the path of non-violence despite the injustices they suffer. The great dream and passion, however, is for a peace in which men can live in a true union of love.

These opening passages of the chapter set the tone, one that is deliberately free from any polemic spirit or any tendency to be concerned with establishing guilt in regard to the troubled times that afflict mankind today. The strong emphasis is on the goal of achieving peace, even though the Council, at the suggestion of some of the fathers, is careful to note that it speaks in praise not of those who merely claim to be seeking peace but of those who are true peacemakers (n. 79).

In taking up the question of avoiding war, the Council fathers turned first to the nature of war and its savage violence today. There is a note of realism about the reference to new modes of warfare with the attendant problems they pose in international law or international relations. On the topic of guerrilla warfare as well as on that of genocide, the document speaks with deep feeling. The text clearly condemns acts of genocide as "horrendous crimes" (n. 79) and praises those who refuse to obey immoral commands issued in the name of a supreme civil or military authority.

Throughout the latter days of debate on the Pastoral Constitution and in particular on this section dealing with war and peace, it was generally reported in the world press that a bloc of vigorous opponents of any statement were making their voices heard in the Council and in sessions of the drafting commission. Some critics of the text argued that the Council could not possibly issue a statement on this theme at this time since the materials were not ready. They urged that the whole matter be dropped or the debate postponed until the synod of bishops could meet after the Council had closed. (It is known that another proposal to amend this section of the Constitution called for the insertion of the address of Pope Paul VI to the United Nations General Assembly on October 4, 1965, in place of the passages dealing with war and peace. The text of that remarkable address was in fact inserted into the record of the Council.) The brief sentence on conscientious objectors in this portion of the text (n. 79) was the sort of controversial statement that caused endless debate. In the final stages of drafting the text, a body of Council fathers requested that this particular statement be deleted, and they provided a number of reasons to justify their request. They regarded it variously as too difficult a subject, too controversial, too specific, or not the business of the Council since it was not clear from natural law. Others objected on the grounds of the evil consequences that flow from civil disobedience and the like. The drafting commission remained firm in its support of the statement as it had been written and as it eventually appeared in the final text. One reason for this firmness was that the statement had in fact been approved in principle by a vast majority of the Council fathers. Moreover, the commission pointed out that the statement as it read made no judgment in the objective moral order on conscientious objection as such. It is worth calling attention to the extent of debate on this single issue in order to emphasize the care with which this portion of the Constitution was considered by all.

If the Pastoral Constitution calls attention to the necessity of humane laws to regulate the case of conscientious objectors, it also makes clear the positive meaning of just defense and speaks with praise of those who serve their country as "the custodians of the security and freedom of their fellow countrymen" (n. 79).

The burden of the document's teaching on war, however, is a passionate concern about the evils of modern warfare and the need to "undertake a completely fresh reappraisal of war" (n. 80). The unique hazard of modern war is that the owner of its almost inconceivable weapons can perpetrate a horror beyond imagination. In a use of the word "condemnation" that is almost unparalleled in the vocabulary of Vatican Council II, the Council fathers characterize total warfare as an act "which merits firm and unequivocal condemnation" (n. 80). (A note in the official records tells us that when some bishops objected to the term "condemnation", the drafting commission simply replied that the word was being used here in a sense which would be completely understood by the men to whom it was addressed.)

The Constitution deals in particular with the problem of the arms race as it exists today. It recognizes the arguments commonly advanced in support of the amassing of new scientific weapons for defensive purposes. Nevertheless, the fathers insist that the accumulation of arms cannot really be accepted as a sound way to preserve a firm peace. Moreover, there is the question of the huge cost, particularly when seen in terms of aid denied because of this spending to those afflicted by miseries of poverty and hunger in the world today. The conclusion of the Council is that "the arms race is one of the greatest curses on the human race" (n. 81). Here again, as with the passage on conscientious objectors, there were a number of quite vocal critics in the Council. Some feared that this harsh analysis of the arms race would be misused by enemies of freedom or prove offensive to the wealthier nations who seemed singled out for criticism; others asserted that it failed to point out the dangers in the arms race even among developing nations. But the great majority of the Council fathers from all nations of the world chose to run the risk of misunderstanding rather than refrain from calling on men to free themselves "from the age-old slavery of war" (n. 81).

It is not the intention of Vatican Council II to call for a heedless effort at unilateral disarmament. The fathers insist that the peace to be sought must be one that is born of mutual trust. It is for this reason that the document summons all men to lend support to leaders of goodwill who genuinely work for peace. The Council fathers pledge their prayers for guidance and strength to be given to these men. They also recognize that there is a heavy responsibility on many, specifically on those involved in the education of the young, to educate men to peace. The private citizen cannot pass off his responsibil- for forming public opinion on behalf of peace.

It is because of this important part played by public opinion that the Council fathers also chose to insist on the continuing individual responsibility of all men as they face the threat of world peace. The private citizen cannot pass off his responsibilities by entrusting every aspect of decisions on the matter of war and peace to public authority. One is reminded here of a statement later issued by the American hierarchy at the close of a national meeting in November 1966: "While we cannot resolve all of the issues involved in the Vietnam conflict, it is clearly our duty to insist that they be kept under constant moral scrutiny. No one is free to evade this personal responsibility by leaving it entirely to others to make moral judgments. In this connection, Vatican Council II warned that 'people should take care not to entrust themselves only to the efforts of others, while remaining careless about their own attitudes. For State leaders . . . rely to a great extent on public opinion and public attitudes'."

In the quest for peace there can be no place for false hopes or for an unrealistic ignoring of the existence of enmities and hatred among men. At the same time, it is impossible to rest content with a pessimistic appraisal of current trends. The risk is that these trends, if left to themselves, will result only in the "dread peace of death" (n. 82).

The task of achieving peace cannot consist merely in avoiding or forestalling war. The Pastoral Constitution is quite clear in declaring the necessity of getting at the roots or causes of international discord. Men and institutions must be concerned with injustices and inequalities, with jealousy, pride and distress, and with the dreadful infection of violence, all of which so often lie at the root of wars or threats of war between nations. "Man should work unsparingly toward the creation of organizations designed to promote the cause of peace" (n. 83).

In a statement that ratifies the line of thought initiated by Pius XII and carried on by his successors, John XXIII and Paul VI, the Council fathers argue from the necessity to achieve a universal common good to the need for international institutions aimed at promoting that worldwide general interest. There must be a real international order, and international agencies, both universal and regional, must exist to preserve and foster that order (n. 84).

Interest in building up genuine international order and peace must move beyond the area of concern for the political independence of men and nations. The Council fathers stress the special problems confronting us in the field of international economic cooperation. Here they emphasize the need for both financial assistance and whatever human aid that can be provided by experts. Anyone familiar with the work of such international Catholic agencies as the Catholic Relief Services of the United States and Misereor and Adveniat in Germany will see that the programs which they have recently instituted are here officially approved by the Council (n. 85).

It may be a matter of interest to note the care with which the significance even of individual words was examined by the Council fathers and the drafting commission. In the section on "International Cooperation in Economic Matters" (n. 85), for instance, it was suggested that in speaking of aid to be offered by advanced nations to those in the process of development, the latter should be urged to accept such aid "with complete honesty and gratitude". The drafting commission, with the subsequent approval of the vast majority of Council fathers, refused to add the word "gratitude" on the score that such aid was a matter of justice and not merely some sort of gift. In a similar context, the commission also rejected a proposal to qualify the word "justice" with the term "distributive", basing its decision on the desire to avoid making too many distinctions.

In going about the task of promoting international economic cooperation, the Pastoral Constitution offers some essential norms. One is that the aim of the developing nations in accepting aid and in putting it to use must be to achieve the complete human fulfillment of all their citizens and to help all to help themselves. For the advanced or developed nations, there is a very serious obligation to adopt a completely new attitude, one that involves actively considering or seeking out the needs of weaker and poorer nations. In order to keep perfectly clear the gravity of this obligation, the drafting commission rejected a proposal to speak of "an obligation of brotherhood and human solidarity". It rejected this proposal because it felt the nature of the obligation would remain too ambiguous and it wanted it clearly understood that the matter was not one of obligation but one of justice (n. 86).

In this matter of economic international cooperation, the fathers note that the international community itself, while respecting the proper functions of lesser agencies or institutions, must take a hand in offering guidance and coordination. However, neither the international community as such nor the advanced or developing nations should ignore the necessity to also reform economic and social structures. The Council offers one important and highly significant caution here when it warns against the adoption of immature plans or proposals. It goes on to make clear that one must always take every precaution to ensure that the heritage of a people is not destroyed by the hasty introduction of ill-conceived plans for economic reform.

One of the most widely discussed and controverted aspects of the overall picture of international economic cooperation is that concerning cooperation on population. The Council fathers explicitly affirm the special need for cooperation of all parties where a country faces rapid population growth and the problems that arise from it. According to the fathers, it is clear that there is a need here to look toward reform of farming methods and the introduction of new social systems. The document also notes the part that government officials and public authorities can and must play in this matter. Pope Paul VI recently summarized the thinking of Vatican Council II on this point in his encyclical, *Progressio populorum:* "It is certain that public authorities can intervene, within the limit of their competence, by favoring the availability of appropriate information and by adopting suitable measures, provided that these be in conformity with the moral law and that they respect the rightful freedom of married couples" (n. 37).

Interestingly enough, the conciliar text calls explicitly for the greater involvement of Catholic experts from the universities and elsewhere in studying the many questions posed by demographic growth and the rapid rise of population. Lest there be any mistake about the Council's concern that Catholics contribute to these studies, the drafting commission refused to accept a modification of the passage in which reference was made to "Catholic" experts (n. 87). It is clear that the Council, as Pope Paul would later do in his encyclical, cautions against morally unacceptable methods or approaches to the population problem and against coercion in the area where individual consciences must prevail. At the same time, the Pastoral Constitution is fully consistent with its own earlier discussion of family morality in sustaining the right of parents to make the ultimate judgment and in affirming the need to inform people about scientific advances in the area of birth regulation. Both in this section and in the earlier treatment of family morality, the Pastoral Constitution has moved in the direction of greater openness to birth regulation as an approach to population growth, thus developing the position spelled out by John XXIII in his encyclical *Mater et Magistra*.

The concluding section of this last chapter of Part II of the Pastoral Constitution deals with the duty of Christians and with the role of the Church herself in promoting international cooperation as the necessary bulwark of international peace. The Council fathers reaffirm the duty of Christians to collaborate willingly in programs aimed at promoting international cooperation. They note the scandal that arises when Christian nations "enjoy an abundance of riches, while others lack the necessities of life and are tortured by hunger, disease and all kinds of misery" (n. 88). They have a word of special praise for all, especially the young, who give service in various agencies concerned with the works of international cooperation, and they recommend that participation by dioceses or other Catholic institutions in giving aid and technical advice should be coordinated as far as possible.

In a special section on the presence of the Church as such on the international scene (n. 89), the Pastoral Constitution reaffirms the Church's right to teach and to be present through her public institutions in the affairs of the world community. The history of the Holy See's active role in UNESCO activities and the programs of other agencies linked with the United Nations is an historical realization of that sense of duty and right. In speaking on this matter of the Church's presence, the fathers also call attention to the need to impart this sense of world responsibility in the education of youth today. This recommendation comes with great timeliness in a period when there is such growing stress on the concept of international education.

Throughout the entire Pastoral Constitution, as well as in other documents of Vatican Council II such as the *Decree on the Apostolate of the Laity,* there is repeated emphasis on the active role that must be played by all Christians in areas such as that of international cooperation and the quest for international justice and peace. In the concluding section of this chapter, the Council fathers praise all who aid international organizations designed to promote these objectives. It mentions particularly those under Catholic auspices. The Council fathers remark, however, that there is also need "to establish an organism of the universal Church whose task would be to arouse the Catholic community to promote the progress of needy regions and to further social justice between nations" (n. 90). Behind this call for a special agency of the universal Church lies a history of effort on the part of interested persons to bring this need to the attention of the Council. For American readers there is special interest in the very active part played by several American prelates and laymen in this particular project. One thinks particularly of Bishop Edward E. Swanstrom, Monsignor Joseph Gremillion and Mr. James J. Norris, all associated with the Catholic Relief Services of the United States. It will be recalled that Mr. Norris, a lay auditor at the Council, had been invited to address the Council in one of the rare speeches given by anyone other than a bishop or superior general. The concrete implementation of this recommendation of the Council and the realization of the proposals of these men and such associates as the distinguished economist, Barbara Ward, came with the formation of a Secretariat for Justice and Peace in Rome. A suggestion had been

made by several of the Council fathers that this
agency be established from the outset on ecumenical lines. The drafting commission rejected such a
proposed emendation of the text of the document
on the grounds that it would be necessary to have a
Catholic agency in existence in order to enter into
dialogue with Protestant and other religious groups
or secular agencies who might be interested in such
cooperation.

VI
CONCLUSION

The closing passages of the Pastoral Constitution deal fittingly with the great need for unity—
unity of vision and aspirations and unity of work in
cooperation. The Council fathers note that their
teaching is addressed both to believers and to non-
believers since they are dealing with questions that
relate to man's full destiny and dignity. They admit
candidly that the "program" (n. 91) they propose
is very general, but at the same time they express
confidence that it can help everyone after the principles are fittingly adapted to concrete situations.
One phrase that provoked some discussion prior to
the final voting on this section of the Constitution
concerned the suggestion that the faithful imple-
ment these proposals "under the direction of their
pastors" (n. 91). In their suggestions for changes in
the text, some of the fathers felt that this statement
appeared to contradict an earlier statement that
"pastors will not always be so expert as to have a
ready answer to every problem" (n. 43). It is interesting to note that in refusing to delete this phrase
the commission insisted that there was no contradiction here. In other words, the full force of the

statement from the earlier part of the Constitution remains. Their purpose in calling attention to the role of pastors in this task of implementing the broad principles of the Constitution is simply to affirm the basic teaching function of pastors in the Church.

As for the Church herself, what is the meaning of this attempt on the part of an ecumenical Council to spell out the Church's sense of her relationship to the modern world? In entering, so to speak, into dialogue with the world, "the Church shows herself as a sign of that spirit of brotherhood by which sincere dialogue is not only made possible but also strengthened" (n. 92). "Dialogue" here is obviously meant in the sense defined at length by Paul VI in the inaugural encyclical of his pontificate, *Ecclesiam suam*. It is a dialogue that is open to all members of the Church herself, to other Christians, and to all other men of goodwill, including non-believers. As the Constitution goes on to remark, this dialogue is open in a special sense even to those who oppress the Church (n. 92). Here one is clearly reminded of the famous passage in John XXIII's *Pacem in terris*: "Meetings and agreements, in the various sectors of daily life, between believers and those who do not believe or believe insufficiently because they adhere to error, can be occasions for discovering truth and paying homage to it" (n. 158).

In a sentence that surely startled many—in fact, there were some Council fathers who asked that it be deleted on the grounds that it tended to favor religious indifferentism—the Constitution sums up this sense of human unity by citing the common brotherhood of men. From this fact it draws the conclusion that since we have been summoned to the same destiny, which is both human and divine, "we must work together without violence and without deceit to build up the world in a spirit of genuine peace" (n. 92).

Perhaps at this point some explicit observations should be made about the ecumenical impact or import of the Pastoral Constitution as such. At a number of points throughout this lengthy document, the Council fathers had been careful to note and give approving mention to the possibility or necessity of cooperation with men of goodwill, particularly with those who share in the Christian faith with Catholics. However, the importance of the document lies not so much in this openness of mind on the part of the framers of the Constitution, but rather in what is concretely proposed in the way of cooperation. This point, it may be noted, had been made by one of the most acute of the Protestant observers at the Council, Dr. Lukas Vischer, a member of the staff of the central headquarters of the World Council of Churches. In a report prepared for a central committee meeting of the World Council of Churches in January 1965, Dr. Vischer said: "It scarcely needs to be emphasized that the schema is extremely important for the ecumenical movement. The problems with which it deals confront the other Churches too in the same or a similar way. The separated Churches find themselves in the present-day world in a dilemma which is common to all of them. Therefore, the Council could take steps here which would bind the Churches together. For it is in the extent to which common answers are successfully found that not only unity as such but also our common witness is furthered."

There is another sense, however, in which the entire *Pastoral Constitution on the Church in the Modern World* is of profound ecumenical significance. This had also been noted by Dr. Vischer in

the report cited above: "Study of the relation between the Church and the world necessarily leads
to a fresh study of the nature of the Church. A discussion on the place of the Church in the modern
world inevitably has ecclesiological implications.
The traditional picture of the Church is called in
question, for the picture which the Church has of
herself comes from another time, a past time in
which the relationship between the Church and the
world presented itself in a quite different light. . . .
Study of the present attitude of the Church to the
world may reveal to us the historical relativity of
many ecclesiological convictions and bring freshly
to our consciousness the original will of Christ."
In a sense, Dr. Vischer here seems to echo one of
the points that Pope John XXIII regarded as a key
objective of Vatican Council II when he spoke of
the work of the Council as achieving a new level of
"self-consciousness" for the Church as a whole. It
remains for theologians and historians to decide to
what extent this new self-understanding, this new
ecclesiological insight, was in fact realized in the
Pastoral Constitution. Clearly the Council fathers,
in the words of the closing general exhortation that
ends the lengthy Constitution, saw a vision of the
Church that is organically linked with that spelled
out in the *Dogmatic Constitution on the Church*.
It is a vision of the Church as a sign, witness and
sacrament. Above all it is a vision of the Church as
servant. In his remarks at the closing ceremony of
the Council on December 7, 1965, Pope Paul said
that in this Constitution "the idea of service has
been central".

De Ecclesia
In Mundo Huius Temporis

THE
PASTORAL CONSTITUTION
ON THE CHURCH
IN THE MODERN WORLD

**Promulgated by Pope Paul VI
December 7, 1965**

PAUL BISHOP

SERVANT OF THE SERVANTS OF GOD
TOGETHER WITH THE FATHERS OF THE SACRED COUNCIL
COMMITS TO PERMANENT RECORD

THE
PASTORAL CONSTITUTION
ON THE CHURCH
IN THE MODERN WORLD[1]

PREFACE

Solidarity of the Church with the Whole Human Family

1. The joy and hope, the grief and anguish of the men of our time, especially those who are poor or afflicted in any way, are the joy and hope, the grief and anguish of the followers of Christ as well. Nothing that is genuinely human fails to find an echo in their hearts, for theirs is a community composed of men who, united in Christ and guided by

---

[1] The *Pastoral Constitution on the Church in the Modern World* is composed of two parts, yet it constitutes an organic unity. It is called "pastoral" because, while resting on doctrinal principles, it seeks to express the relation of the Church to the world and modern mankind. As a result, the emphasis is pastoral in Part I and doctrinal in Part II. In Part I, the Church develops her teaching on man, on the world which is the enveloping context of man's existence,

the Holy Spirit, press onward toward the kingdom of the Father and are bearers of a message of salvation intended for all men. That is the reason why Christians cherish a feeling of deep solidarity with the human race and its history.

The Council Addresses All Men

2. Now that Vatican Council II has deeply studied the mystery of the Church, it resolutely addresses not only the sons of the Church and all who invoke the name of Christ, but the whole of humanity as well, and it longs to set forth the way it understands the presence and function of the Church in the modern world.

Therefore, the world which the Council has in mind is the whole human family seen in the context of everything which envelops it. It is the world as the theater of human history, bearing the marks of man's travail, his triumphs and his failures. It is the world which, in the Christian vision, has been created and is sustained by the love of its creator. It is the world which has been freed from the slavery of sin by Christ who was crucified and rose again in order to break the stranglehold of the Evil One so that it might be fashioned anew according to God's design and brought to its fulfillment.

and on man's relations with his fellowmen. In Part II, the Church gives closer consideration to various aspects of modern life and human society, especially to those questions and problems which, in this general area, seem to have a greater urgency in our day. As a result, in Part II the subject matter which is viewed in the light of doctrinal principles is made up of diverse elements. Some of these elements have a permanent value while others are only transitory. Consequently, this Constitution must be interpreted according to the general norms of theological interpretation. Interpreters must bear in mind, especially in Part II, the changeable circumstances which the subject matter, by its very nature, involves.

An Offer of Service to Mankind

3. In a state of wonder at their own discoveries and their own might, men of today are troubled and perplexed by questions about current trends in the world, about their place and their role in the universe, about the meaning of individual and collective endeavor and, finally, about the destiny of nature and of men. And so the Council, as witness for and guide to the faith of the whole People of God gathered together by Christ, can find no more eloquent expression of its solidarity and respectful affection for the whole human family to which it belongs than to enter into dialogue with this family about all these different problems. The Council will clarify these problems in the light of the Gospel and furnish mankind with the saving resources which the Church has received from her founder under the promptings of the Holy Spirit. It is man himself who must be saved; it is mankind that must be renewed. It is man, therefore, who is the key to this discussion—man considered whole and entire, with body and soul, heart and conscience, mind and will.

This is the reason why this sacred Synod, in proclaiming the noble destiny of man and perceiving an element of the divine in him, offers to cooperate unreservedly with all men in fostering a sense of brotherhood to correspond to this destiny of theirs. The Church is not motivated by any earthly ambition but is interested in one thing only—to carry on the work of Christ under the guidance of the Holy Spirit, for he came into the world to bear witness to the truth, to save and not to judge, to serve and not to be served.[2]

---

[2] Cf. Jn. 3, 17; 18, 37; Mt. 20, 28; Mk. 10, 45.

INTRODUCTION

THE SITUATION OF MAN IN THE MODERN WORLD

Hope and Anguish

4. At all times the Church has the responsibility of scrutinizing the signs of the times and of interpreting them in the light of the Gospel if she is to carry out her task. In language intelligible to every generation, she should be able to answer the ever recurring questions that men ask about the meaning of this present life and of the life to come and about how one is related to the other. We must be aware of and understand the aspirations, the yearnings and the often dramatic features of the world in which we live. An outline of some of the more important features of the modern world forms the subject matter of the following paragraphs.

Ours is a new age of history, with critical and swift upheavals spreading gradually to all corners of the earth. They are the products of man's intelligence and creative activity, but they recoil upon him, upon his judgments and desires, both individual and collective, and upon his ways of thinking and acting in regard to people and things. We are entitled, then, to speak of a social and cultural transformation whose repercussions are also felt on the religious level.

A transformation of this kind brings up the serious problems associated with any crisis of growth. Increase in power is not always accompanied by control of that power for the benefit of man. In probing the recesses of his own mind, man often seems more uncertain of himself than ever; in the gradual and precise unfolding of the laws of social living, he is perplexed by uncertainty about how to plot its course.

In no other age has mankind enjoyed such an abundance of wealth, resources and economic well-being, and yet an overwhelming proportion of the population is still tortured by hunger and almost total illiteracy. At no time have men had such a keen sense of freedom, only to be faced by new forms of slavery in living and thinking. There is, on the one hand, a lively feeling of unity and of the compelling solidarity of mutual dependence, and, on the other, a lamentable cleavage of bitterly opposed camps. We have not yet seen the last of bitter political, social and economic hostility or racial and ideological antagonism, nor are we free from the specter of a war of total destruction. If there is a growing exchange of ideas, there is still widespread disagreement about the meaning of the words expressing our key concepts. There is, lastly, a painstaking search for a better material world, but without a parallel spiritual advancement.

It is small wonder, then, that many of our contemporaries are prevented by this complex situation from recognizing permanent values and duly applying them to recent discoveries. As a result they hover between hope and despair and wonder uneasily about the present course of events. It is a situation that challenges men to reply; they cannot escape.

Deep-Seated Changes

5. The spiritual uneasiness of today and the changing structure of life are part of a broader upheaval clearly indicated by the increasing part played on the intellectual level by the mathematical sciences (not excluding the sciences dealing with man himself) and on the practical level by their repercussions on technology. The scientific mentality has wrought a change in the cultural sphere and on habits of thought, and the progress of technology is now reshaping the face of the earth and has its sights set on the conquest of space.

The human mind is, in a certain sense, broadening its mastery over time—over the past through the insights of history and over the future by foresight and planning. Advances in biology, psychology and the social sciences not only lead man to greater self-awareness, but also provide him with the technical means of molding the lives of whole peoples as well. At the same time the human race is giving more and more thought to the forecasting and control of its own demographic expansion.

The accelerated pace of history is such that one can scarcely keep abreast of it. Hitherto the destiny of mankind as a whole consisted of the fragmentary annals of various peoples; now it merges into a complete whole. And so, mankind substitutes a dynamic and more evolutionary concept of nature for a static one, and the result is an immense series of new problems calling for a new endeavor of analysis and synthesis.

Changes in the Social Order

6. As a result the traditional structure of local communities—family, clan, tribe, village, various groupings and social relationships—is subjected to

ever more sweeping changes. Industrialization is on the increase; it has raised some nations to a position of affluence, and at the same time it has radically transfigured ideas and social practices hallowed for centuries. Urbanization is also on the increase, both on account of the expanding number of city dwellers and the spread of an urban way of life into rural settings. New and more efficient mass media are contributing to the spread of knowledge and the extensive diffusion of habits of thought and feeling, setting off chain reactions in their wake. One cannot underestimate the effect of emigration on those who, for whatever reason, are led to undertake a new way of life. On the whole, the bonds uniting man to his fellowmen multiply without ceasing, and "socialization" creates yet other bonds, without, however, a corresponding personal development and truly personal relationships ("personalization"). It is above all in countries with advanced standards of economic and social progress that these developments are evident, but there are stirrings for advancement among peoples eager to share in the benefits of industrialization and urbanization. Such peoples, especially where ancient traditions are still strong, are at the same time conscious of the need to exercise their freedom in a more mature and personal way.

Changes in Attitudes, Morals and Religion

7. Controversy about accepted values often follows the changing of attitudes and structures; this is true, above all, in the case of young people, whose occasional impatience and at times anguished rebellion urges them to aspire to premature participation in the life of society where they are conscious of their special influence. It is no surprise that parents and teachers are finding it more

difficult every day to carry out their duties. **Behavior** and its guiding norms are in a state of confusion because the framework of laws and inherited ideas and attitudes does not always seem to be in line with the modern rhythm of life.

As regards religion, there is a completely new atmosphere that conditions its practice. On the one hand, people are taking a hard look at all magical world views and prevailing superstitions and demanding a more personal and active commitment of faith; as a result, many people have achieved a lively sense of the divine. On the other hand, greater numbers are falling away from the practice of religion. In the past it was the exception to repudiate God and religion to the point of abandoning them—and such occurred only in individual cases—but nowadays it seems a matter of course to reject them as incompatible with scientific progress and a new kind of humanism. In many places it is not only in philosophical terms that such trends are expressed, but there are signs of them in literature, art, the humanities, the interpretation of history and even civil law. All of this is very disturbing to many people.

Imbalances in the World of Today

8. The rapid development of the world and a keener awareness of existing inequalities have resulted in the creation and aggravation of differences and imbalances. On the personal level there often arises an imbalance between an outlook which is practical and modern and a way of thinking which fails to master and synthesize the sum total of its ideas. Another imbalance occurs between the demands of practicality and the scruples of conscience, not to mention that between the claims of group living and the needs of individual reflection

and contemplation. A third imbalance takes the form of conflict between specialization and an over-all view of reality.

On the family level there are tensions arising out of demographic, economic and social conditions, out of conflicts between succeeding generations, and out of new social relationships between the sexes.

On the level of race and social class we find tensions between the affluent and the underdeveloped nations; we find them between international bodies established in the interests of peace and the ambitions of ideological indoctrination with the goal of national or bloc expansionism. In the midst of it all stands man, at once the author and the victim of mutual distrust, animosity, conflict and woe.

Broader Aspirations of Mankind

9.   Meanwhile, there is a growing conviction of mankind's ability and duty to strengthen its mastery over nature and of the need to establish a political, social and economic order at the service of man to assert and develop the dignity proper to individuals and to societies. Great numbers of people are acutely conscious of being deprived of the world's goods through injustice and unfair distribution and are vehemently demanding to share in them. Developing nations, such as those who have recently gained their independence, are anxious to share in the political and economic benefits of modern civilization and to play their part freely in the world, but they are hampered by their economic dependence on the rapidly expanding richer nations and the ever widening gap between them. The hungry nations cry out to their affluent neighbors; where women have not already obtained

parity with men, they claim it as fact and demand it as their right; farmers and workers insist on a minimum standard of living plus the opportunity to develop their personal talents and play their due role in organizing economic, social, political and cultural life. Now for the first time in history people are not afraid to think that cultural benefits are for all and should be available to everyone.

These claims are but the sign of a deeper and more widespread aspiration. Man as an individual and as a member of society craves a life that is full, autonomous and worthy of his nature as a human being; he longs to harness for his own purposes the immense resources of the modern world. Among nations there is a growing movement to set up a worldwide community.

In the light of the foregoing factors there appears the dichotomy of a world that is at once powerful and weak, capable of doing what is noble and what is base, disposed to freedom and slavery, progress and decline, brotherhood and hatred. Man is growing conscious of the fact that the forces he has unleashed are in his own hands and that it is up to him to control them or be enslaved by them. Here lies the modern dilemma.

Man's Deeper Questionings

10. The dichotomy affecting the modern world is, in fact, a symptom of the deeper dichotomy that is in man himself. He is the meeting point of many conflicting forces. In his condition as a created being he is subject to a thousand shortcomings, but he feels untrammeled in his inclinations and destined for a higher form of life. Torn by a welter of anxieties he is compelled to choose between them and repudiate some. Worse still, feeble and sinful as he is, he often does the very

thing he hates and does not do what he prefers.[3] And so, he feels himself divided, and the result is a host of discords in social life. Many unfortunately fail to see the dramatic nature of this state of affairs in all its clarity, for their vision is blurred on the practical level by materialism, or they are prevented from even thinking about it by the wretchedness of their plight. Others delude themselves that they have found peace in a world view now fashionable. There are still others who hope to achieve a genuine and total emancipation of mankind through human effort alone and who look forward to some future paradise where all the desires of their hearts will be fulfilled. Nor is it unusual to find people who, having lost faith in life, extol the kind of foolhardiness which would empty life of any inherent significance and invest it with a meaning of their own devising. Nonetheless, in the face of modern developments there is a growing body of men who are asking the most fundamental of all questions or are glimpsing them with a keener insight: What is man? What is the meaning of suffering, evil and death which have not been eliminated by all this progress? Are these achievements worth the price that has to be paid? What can man contribute to society? What can he expect from it? What happens after this earthly life is ended?

The Church believes that Christ, who died and was raised for the sake of all,[4] can show man the way and strengthen him through the Spirit in order that he may be worthy of his destiny. There is no other name under heaven given to men by which they must be saved.[5] The Church likewise believes

---

3 Cf. Rom. 7, 14ff.

4 Cf. 2 Cor. 5, 15.

5 Cf. Acts 4, 12.

that the key, the center and the purpose of the whole of man's history is to be found in her Lord and master. She also maintains that in all these upheavals there is much that is unchanging and much that has its ultimate foundation in Christ, who is the same yesterday and today and forever.[6] That is why the Council, relying on the inspiration of Christ, the image of the invisible God, the firstborn of all creation,[7] proposes to speak to all men in order to unfold the mystery that is man and cooperate in tackling the main problems facing the world today.

---

[6] Cf. Heb. 13, 8.
[7] Cf. Col. 1, 15.

PART I

THE CHURCH AND MAN'S VOCATION

Response to the Promptings of the Holy Spirit

11. The People of God believes that it is led by the Spirit of the Lord who fills the whole world. Moved by that faith it tries to discern what may be genuine signs of the presence or the purpose of God in the events, the needs and the longings which it shares with other men of our time. For faith throws a new light on all things and makes known the full ideal which God has set for man, thus guiding the mind toward solutions that are fully human.

In that light the Council intends, first of all, to form a judgment on those values which are most highly prized today and to relate them to their divine source. Such values, insofar as they stem from the natural talents given to man by God, are exceedingly good. However, owing to corruption of the human heart, they are often distorted through lack of due order, so that they need to be placed in their proper perspective.

What does the Church think of man? What measures deserve approval for building up society today? What is the final meaning of man's activity in the universe? These questions call for a reply.

From their answers it will be increasingly clear that the People of God and the human race which is its setting render service to each other; thus the mission of the Church will show itself to be supremely human by the very fact of being religious.

CHAPTER I

THE DIGNITY OF THE HUMAN PERSON

Man as the Image of God

12. Believers and unbelievers agree almost unanimously that all things on earth should be ordained to man as to their center and summit. But what is man? He has put forward, and continues to do so, many views about himself, views that are different and even opposed to each other. Often he either sets himself up as the absolute measure of all things or debases himself to the point of despair—hence his doubt and his anguish. The Church is keenly sensitive to these difficulties. Enlightened by divine revelation, she can offer a solution to them by which the true state of man may be outlined and his weakness explained in such a way that at the same time his dignity and his vocation may be perceived in their true light.

Sacred Scripture teaches that man was created "in the image of God", able to know and love his creator, and appointed by him over all earthly creatures [8] that he might rule them and make use of them while glorifying God.[9] "What is man that thou art mindful of him, and the Son of man that

[8] Cf. Gen. 1, 26; Wis. 2, 23.
[9] Cf. Sir. 17, 3-10.

thou dost care for him? Yet thou hast made him little less than God, and dost crown him with glory and honor. Thou hast given him dominion over the works of thy hands; thou hast put all things under his feet" (Ps. 8, 5-8).

But God did not create man as a solitary being. From the beginning "male and female he created them" (Gen. 1, 27). This partnership of man and woman constitutes the first form of communion between persons. By his innermost nature man is a social being, and if he does not enter into relations with others, he can neither live nor develop his gifts.

Therefore, as we read elsewhere in the Bible, God saw "all the things that he had made, and they were very good" (Gen. 1, 31).

Sin

13.   Although set by God in a state of rectitude, man, enticed by the Evil One, abused his freedom at the very start of history. He lifted himself up against God and sought to attain his goal apart from him. Although he had known God, he did not glorify him as God, but his senseless heart was darkened and he served the creature rather than the creator.[10]

What revelation makes known to us is confirmed by our own experience. For when man looks into his own heart, he finds that he is drawn toward what is wrong, and he sinks into many evils which cannot come from his good creator. Often refusing to acknowledge God as his source, man has also upset the relationship which should link him to his last end; at the same time he has broken the right order that should reign within himself as

---

10 Cf. Rom. 1, 21-25.

well as between himself and other men and all creatures.

Man therefore is divided in himself. As a result, the whole life of men, both individual and social, shows itself to be a dramatic struggle between good and evil, between light and darkness. Man finds that by himself he is unable to overcome the assaults of evil successfully; thus he feels as though he is bound by chains. But the Lord himself came to free and strengthen man, renewing him inwardly and casting out the "prince of this world" (Jn. 12, 31) who held him in the bondage of sin.[11] For sin brought man to a lower state, forcing him away from the completeness that is his to attain. Both the high calling and the deep misery which men experience find their ultimate explanation in the light of divine revelation.

The Essential Nature of Man

14. Man, though composed of body and soul, is a unity. Through his very bodily condition he sums up in himself the elements of the material world. Through him they are thus brought to their highest perfection and can raise their voice in praise freely given to the creator.[12] For this reason man may not despise his bodily life. Rather, he is obliged to regard his body as good and to hold it in honor since God has created it and will raise it up on the last day. Nevertheless, man has been wounded by sin. He finds by experience that his body is in revolt. His very dignity therefore requires that he should glorify God in his body[13] and not allow it to serve the evil inclinations of his heart.

Man is not deceived when he regards himself as

[11] Cf. Jn. 8, 34.
[12] Cf. Dan. 3, 57-90.
[13] Cf. 1 Cor. 6, 13-20.

superior to bodily things and as more than just a speck of nature or a nameless unity in the city of man. For by his power to know himself in the depths of his being he rises above the whole universe of mere objects. When he is drawn to think about his real self, he turns to those deep recesses of his being where God, who probes the heart,[14] awaits him, and where he himself decides his own destiny in the sight of God. Therefore, when he recognizes that his soul is spiritual and immortal, he is not being led astray by false imaginings that are due to merely physical or social causes. On the contrary, he grasps what is profoundly true in this matter.

Dignity of the Intellect, of Truth and of Wisdom

15.   Sharing in the light of the divine mind, man rightly affirms that by his intellect he surpasses the world of mere things. By diligent use of his talents through the ages he has indeed made progress in the empirical sciences, in technology and in the liberal arts. In our time his attempts to search out the secrets of the material universe and to bring it under his control have been extremely successful. Yet he has always looked for, and found, truths of a higher order, for his intellect is not confined to the range of what can be observed by the senses. It can, with genuine certainty, reach to realities known only to the mind, even though, as a result of sin, its vision has been clouded and its powers weakened.

The intellectual nature of man finally finds its perfection, as it should, in wisdom which gently draws the human mind to look for and to love what is true and good. Filled with wisdom, man is led

---

14 Cf. 1 Kgs. 16, 7; Jer. 17, 10.

through visible realities to those which cannot be seen.

Our age, more than any of the past, needs such wisdom if all that man discovers is to be ennobled through human effort. Indeed, the future of the world is in danger unless provision is made for men of greater wisdom. It should also be pointed out that many nations—poorer as far as material goods are concerned, yet richer as regards wisdom—can be of the greatest advantage to others.

It is by the gift of the Holy Spirit that man comes through faith to contemplate and savor the mystery of God's design.[15]

Dignity of Moral Conscience

16. Deep within his conscience man discovers a law which he has not laid upon himself but which he must obey. Its voice, ever calling him to love and to do what is good and avoid evil, tells him inwardly at the right moment to do this or to shun that. For man has in his heart a law inscribed by God. His dignity lies in observing this law, and by it he will be judged.[16] Conscience is man's most secret core, and his sanctuary. There he is alone with God whose voice echoes in his depths.[17] In a wonderful manner, conscience reveals that law which is fulfilled in the love of God and one's neighbor.[18] Through fidelity to conscience Christians are joined to other men in the search for truth and the right solution to so many moral prob-

---

15 Cf. Sir. 17, 7-8.

16 Cf. Rom. 2, 15-16.

17 Cf. Pius XII, Radio Address *On the Correct Formation of a Christian Conscience in the Young,* March 23, 1952: *A.A.S.* 44 (1952), p. 271.

18 Cf. Mt. 22, 37-40; Gal. 5, 14.

lems which arise both in the life of individuals and from social relationships. Hence, the more a correct conscience prevails, the more do persons and groups turn aside from blind choice and seek to be guided by the objective standards of moral conduct. Yet it often happens that conscience goes astray through ignorance which it is unable to avoid, but under such circumstances it does not lose its dignity. This cannot be said of the man who takes little trouble to find out what is true and good, or when conscience is by degrees almost blinded through the habit of committing sin.

The Excellence of Freedom

17.   It is only in freedom, however, that man can turn himself toward what is good. The people of our time prize freedom very highly and strive eagerly to attain it. They are right to do so, yet they often cherish their freedom improperly as if it gave them leave to do anything they like, even if it should be evil. But that which is truly freedom is an exceptional sign of the image of God in man. For God willed that man should "be left in the hand of his own counsel" [19] so that he might of his own accord seek his creator and freely attain his full and blessed perfection by cleaving to him. Man's dignity therefore requires him to act out of conscious and free choice, as moved and drawn in a personal way from within, and not by blind impulses in himself or by mere external constraint. Man gains such dignity when, freeing himself from all slavery to his passions, he presses forward toward his goal by freely choosing what is good and uses his diligence and skill to effectively secure for himself the means suited to this end. Since human

---

[19] Cf. Sir. 15, 14.

freedom has been weakened by sin, it is only by the help of God's grace that man can give his actions their full and proper relationship to God. Before the judgment seat of God, an account of his own life will be rendered to each one according to whether he has done good or evil.[20]

The Mystery of Death

18.   It is in regard to death that man's condition is most shrouded in doubt. Man is tormented not only by pain and by the gradual breaking up of his body but also, and even more, by the dread of forever ceasing to exist. But a deep instinct leads him rightly to shrink from and to reject the utter ruin and total loss of his personality. Because he bears in himself the seed of eternity, which cannot be reduced to mere matter, he rebels against death. All the aids made available by technology, however useful they may be, cannot set his anguished mind at rest. They may prolong his life span, but this does not satisfy his heartfelt longing for a life to come—a longing that can never be stifled.

While the mind is at a loss before the mystery of death, the Church, taught by divine revelation, declares that God has created man for a blessed destiny that lies beyond the limits of his sad state on earth. Moreover, the Christian faith teaches that bodily death, from which man would have been immune had he not sinned,[21] will be overcome when that wholeness which he lost through his own fault will be given to him once again by the almighty and merciful Savior. For God has called man—and continues to call him—to cleave to him with all his being and to share forever a life that is divine and free from all decay. Christ

20 Cf. 2 Cor. 5, 10.
21 Cf. Wis. 1, 13; 2, 23-24; Rom. 5, 21; 6, 23; Jas. 1, 15.

won this victory when he rose to life, for by his own death he freed man from death.[22] Therefore faith, with its solidly based teaching, provides every thoughtful man with an answer to his anxious queries about his future lot. At the same time faith makes him able to be united in Christ with his loved ones who have already died and arouses the hope that they have found true life with God.

Kinds of Atheism and Its Causes

19.   The dignity of man rests above all on the fact that he is called to communion with God. The invitation to converse with God is addressed to man as soon as he comes into being. The reason for man's existence is that God has created him through love, and through love he continues to hold him in that state. He cannot live fully according to truth unless he freely acknowledges that love and entrusts himself to his creator. However, many of our contemporaries either do not perceive, or else explicitly reject, this intimate and vital bond of man to God. Atheism must therefore be regarded as one of the most serious problems of our time, and one that deserves more thorough treatment.

The word "atheism" is used to signify things that differ considerably from one another. Some people expressly deny the existence of God. Others maintain that man cannot make any assertion whatsoever about him. Still others admit only such methods of investigation as would make it seem quite meaningless to ask questions about God. Many, trespassing beyond the boundaries of the positive sciences, either contend that everything can be explained by the reasoning process used in

---

[22] Cf. 1 Cor. 15, 56-57.

such sciences or hold the contrary view that there is no such thing as absolute truth. With some, it is their exaggerated idea of man that causes their faith to languish; they are more prone, it would seem, to affirm man than to deny God. Yet others have such a faulty notion of God that when they disown this product of the imagination, their denial has no reference to the God of the gospels. There are also those who never inquire about God; religion never seems to trouble or interest them at all, nor do they see why they should bother about it. Not infrequently atheism is born from a violent protest against the evil in the world, or from the fact that certain human ideals are wrongfully invested with such an absolute character as to be taken for God. Modern civilization itself can often make it more difficult to approach God, not for any inherent reason, but rather because it is too engrossed in the concerns of this world.

Without doubt, those who willfully try to drive God from their hearts and to avoid all questions about religion, refusing to follow the biddings of their conscience, are not free from blame. But believers themselves often share some responsibility for this situation, for atheism, taken as a whole, is not present in the mind of man from the start. It springs from various causes, among which must be included a critical reaction against religions and, in some places, against the Christian religion in particular. Believers can thus have more than a little to do with the rise of atheism. To the extent that they are careless about their instruction in the faith, or present its teaching falsely, or even fail in their religious, moral or social life, they must be said to conceal rather than to reveal the true nature of God and of religion.

Systematic Atheism

20. Modern atheism frequently takes on a systematic form which, in addition to other causes, so insists on man's desire for autonomy as to object to any dependence on God at all. Those who profess this kind of atheism maintain that freedom consists in the belief that man is an end to himself; he is the sole author of his own history over which he has supreme control. They claim that this outlook cannot be reconciled with the assertion of a Lord who is the author and end of all things, or that at least it makes such an affirmation altogether unnecessary. The sense of power which modern technical progress begets in man may encourage this outlook.

Among the various kinds of present-day atheism, one should take careful note of that variation which looks for man's autonomy through his economic and social emancipation. This form holds that religion of its very nature thwarts such emancipation by arousing man's hopes in a future life, thus both deceiving him and discouraging him from working for a better form of life on earth. As a result, whenever those who hold such views gain control of the State, they violently attack religion; moreover, in order to spread atheism, especially in the education of young people, they make use of all the means by which civil authority can bring pressure to bear on its subjects.

The Attitude of the Church toward Atheism

21. The Church, because of her obligation to both God and man, cannot cease repudiating—with sorrow, yet with the utmost firmness, as she has done in the past [23]—those harmful teachings

23 Cf Pius XI, Encyclical Letter *Divini redemptoris*, March 19, 1937: *A.A.S.* 29 (1937), pp. 65-106; Pius XII, Encyclical

and ways of acting which are in conflict with reason and with common human experience, and which cast man down from the noble state to which he is born. Nevertheless, she tries to seek out the secret motives which lead the atheistic mind to deny God. Well aware how important are the problems raised by atheism, and impelled to act because of her love for all men, she considers that these motives deserve an earnest and more thorough scrutiny.

The Church holds that to acknowledge God is in no way to oppose the dignity of man, since such dignity is grounded and brought to perfection in God. Man has in fact been placed in society by God who created him as an intelligent and free being; but over and above this he is called as a son to intimacy with God and to share in his happiness. She further teaches that hope in a life to come does not take away from the importance of the duties of this life on earth but rather adds to it by giving new motives for fulfilling those duties. On the other hand, when man is left without this divine support and without hope of eternal life, his dignity is deeply wounded, as may so often be seen today. The problems of life and death, of guilt and of suffering, remain unsolved, so that men are frequently cast into despair.

Meanwhile, every man remains a question to himself, one that is dimly perceived and left unanswered. For there are times, especially in the major events of life, when no man can altogether escape from such self-questioning. Only God, who

---

Letter *Ad apostolorum principis,* June 29, 1958: *A.A.S.* 50 (1958), pp. 601-14; John XXIII, Encyclical Letter *Mater et Magistra,* May 15, 1961: *A.A.S.* 53 (1961), pp. 451-53; Paul VI, Encyclical Letter *Ecclesiam suam,* Aug. 6, 1964: *A.A.S.* 56 (1964), pp. 651-53.

calls man to deeper thought and to more humble probing, can fully and with complete certainty supply an answer to this questioning.

Atheism must be countered both by presenting true teaching in a fitting manner and by the full and complete life of the Church and of her members. For it is the function of the Church to render God the Father and his incarnate Son present and, as it were, visible, while ceaselessly renewing and purifying herself under the guidance of the Holy Spirit.[24] This is brought about chiefly by the witness of a living and mature faith—one so well formed that it can see difficulties clearly and overcome them. Many martyrs have borne a splendid witness to this faith and continue to do so. This faith should show its fruitfulness by penetrating the whole life, even the worldly activities, of those who believe, and by urging them to be loving and just, especially toward those in need. Lastly, what most clearly indicates God's presence is the brotherly love of the faithful who, being of one mind and spirit, work together for the faith of the Gospel[25] and present themselves as a sign of unity.

Although the Church completely rejects atheism, she nevertheless sincerely proclaims that all men, believers and unbelievers alike, should help to establish right order in this world where all live together. This certainly cannot be done without sincere and prudent dialogue. The Church therefore deplores any discrimination, whether against believers or unbelievers, which some civil authorities unjustly practice in defiance of the fundamental rights of the human person. She demands effective freedom for the faithful to be allowed to

24 Cf. Vatican Council II. *Dogmatic Constitution on the Church*, n. 8: *A.A.S.* 57 (1965), p. 12.
25 Cf. Phil. 1, 27.

build up God's temple in this world also, and she courteously invites atheists to weigh the merits of the Gospel of Christ with an open mind.

The Church knows full well that her message is in harmony with the most secret desires of the human heart, since it champions the dignity of man's calling, giving hope once more to those who already despair of their higher destiny. Her message, far from impairing man, helps his development by bestowing light, life and freedom. Apart from this message nothing is able to satisfy the heart of man: "Thou hast made us for thyself, O Lord, and our hearts are restless until they rest in thee." [26]

Christ, the New Man

22. In reality it is only in the mystery of the Word made flesh that the mystery of man truly becomes clear. Adam, the first man, was a type of him who was to come,[27] Christ the Lord. Christ, the new Adam, in the revelation of the mystery of the Father and his love, fully reveals man to himself and brings to light his supreme calling. It is no wonder, then, that all the aforementioned truths should find in him their source and their most perfect embodiment.

He who is the "image of the invisible God" (Col. 1, 15) [28] is himself the perfect man who has restored in the children of Adam that likeness to God which had been disfigured ever since the first

---

26 Cf. St. Augustine, *Confessions* 1, 1: *P.L.* 32, 661.
27 Cf. Rom. 5, 14; also cf. Tertullian, *De carnis resurrectione* 6: "The shape that the slime of the earth was given was molded with a view to Christ, the future man": *P.L.* 2, 282; *C.S.E.L.* 47, p. 33, ll. 12-13.
28 Cf. 2 Cor. 4, 4.

sin. Human nature, by the very fact that it was assumed, not absorbed,[29] in him, has also been raised in us to an incomparable dignity. For, by his incarnation, the Son of God has in a certain way united himself with each man. He worked with human hands. He thought with a human mind. He acted with a human will [30] and loved with a human heart. Born of the Virgin Mary, he has truly been made one of us, like us in all respects except sin.[31]

As an innocent lamb he merited life for us by his blood which he freely shed. In him God reconciled us to himself and to one another,[32] freeing us from the bondage of the devil and of sin, so that each one of us could say with the apostle: "The Son of God loved me and gave himself for me" (Gal. 2, 20). By suffering for us he not only gave us an example so that we might follow in his footsteps,[33] but he also opened up a way. If we follow this path, life and death are made holy and acquire a new meaning.

Conformed to the image of the Son who is the firstborn of many brothers,[34] the Christian man

---

29 Cf. Council of Constantinople II, Can. 7: "The divine Word was not changed into a human nature, nor was a human nature absorbed by the Word": *Denz.* 219 (428). Cf. also Council of Constantinople III: "His most holy and immaculate human nature, though deified, was not destroyed (*theótheisa ouk anèrethè*), but rather remained in its proper state and mode of being": *Denz.* 291 (556). Cf. Council of Chalcedon: ". . . to be acknowledged in two natures, without confusion, change, division or separation": *Denz.* 148 (302).

30 Cf. Council of Constantinople III: ". . . and so his human will, though deified, is not destroyed": *Denz.* 291 (556).

31 Cf. Heb. 4, 15.

32 Cf. 2 Cor. 5, 18-19; Col. 1, 20-22.

33 Cf. 1 Pet. 2, 21; Mt. 16, 24; Lk. 14, 27.

34 Cf. Rom. 8, 29; Col. 3, 10-14.

receives the "firstfruits of the Spirit" (Rom. 8, 23) by which he is able to fulfill the new law of love.[35] By this Spirit, who is the "pledge of our inheritance" (Eph. 1, 14), the whole man is inwardly renewed, right up to the "redemption of the body" (Rom. 8, 23). "If the Spirit of him who raised Jesus from the dead dwells in you, he who raised Christ Jesus from the dead will give life to your mortal bodies also through his Spirit who dwells in you" (Rom. 8, 11).[36] The Christian is certainly bound both by need and by duty to struggle with evil through many afflictions and to suffer death, but as one who has been made a partner in the paschal mystery, and as one who has been configured to the death of Christ, he will go forward, strengthened by hope, to the resurrection.[37]

This sharing in Christ's resurrection holds true not only for Christians but also for all men of goodwill in whose hearts grace is active invisibly.[38] For, since Christ died for all,[39] and since all men are in fact called to one and the same divine destiny, we must hold that the Holy Spirit offers to all the possibility of being made partners in the paschal mystery in a way known only to God.

Such is the nature and the greatness of the mystery of man as enlightened for the faithful by the Christian revelation. It is therefore through Christ, and in Christ, that light is cast on the riddles of suffering and death which, apart from his Gospel, overwhelm us. Christ has risen again, destroying death by his death. He has given life to

---

35 Cf. Rom. 8, 1-11.
36 Cf. 2 Cor. 4, 14.
37 Cf. Phil. 3, 10; Rom. 8, 17.
38 Cf. Vatican Council, II, *Dogmatic Constitution on the Church,* n. 16: *A.A.S.* 57 (1965), p. 20.
39 Cf. Rom. 8, 32.

us in abundance [40] so that, becoming sons in the Son, we may cry out in the Spirit: "Abba, Father!" [41]

---

[40] Cf. *The Byzantine Easter Liturgy.*
[41] Cf. Rom. 8, 15; Gal. 4, 6; cf. also Jn. 1, 22; 3, 1-2.

Study-Club Questions

1. Why do people who have only superficial contact with the Church think that she holds a misguided view of man? How does their opinion differ from the Christian anthropology presented in the Constitution?

2. In what way does the Church offer a solution to the conflicting attitudes man has of himself today?

3. Conscience is referred to as a "law" which man has not laid upon himself, but which comes from God and is written in man's heart. What exactly is this "law"? Can man know its prescriptions in advance? Discuss.

4. Only a truly free man can develop a moral conscience. Explain. What is the relation of freedom to conscience?

5. Some think that freedom is the capacity to be able to do whatever one wishes, whereas others see it in terms of being able to do what one should. Can one equate personal freedom with license? With personal responsibility?

6. Conscience is "the core of man's inner life where he is in dialogue with God". Explain.

7. In what way is man's conscience his pathway to the transcendent in his life?

8. Of all the creatures on earth, man is apparently the only one torn between a high calling and the depths of misery. Why do you think man is thus singled out? Does it tell us anything of his vocation in life?

9. In what way do we say that Christ is present in humanity through his incarnation?

10. What can we hope to accomplish through confrontation and dialogue with atheists?

CHAPTER II

The Community of Mankind

Intention of the Council

23. One of the most striking features of today's world is the intense development of interpersonal relationships due in no small measure to modern technical advances. Nevertheless, genuine fraternal dialogue is not advanced so much on this level, but rather at the deeper level of personal fellowship, and this demands mutual respect for the full spiritual dignity of men as persons. Christian revelation contributes greatly to the establishment of this fellowship and at the same time promotes deeper understanding of the laws of social living with which the creator has endowed man's spiritual and moral nature.

Some recent pronouncements of the Church's magisterium have treated at length the Christian teaching about human society; [42] this Council, therefore, proposes to repeat only a few of the more important truths and outline the basis of these

---

[42] Cf. John XXIII, Encyclical Letter *Mater et Magistra,* May 15, 1961: *A.A.S.* 53 (1961), pp. 401-64; John XXIII, Encyclical Letter *Pacem in terris,* April 11, 1963: *A.A.S.* 55 (1963), pp. 257-304; Paul VI, Encyclical Letter *Ecclesiam suam,* Aug. 6, 1964: *A.A.S.* 54 (1964), pp. 609-59.

truths in the light of revelation. Later it will deal
with some of their implications which have special
importance for our day.

Communitarian Nature of Man's Vocation: Design of God

24.   In his fatherly care for all of us, God desired that all men should form one family and deal
with each one another in a spirit of brotherhood.
All, in fact, are destined to the very same end—
namely, God himself—since they have been created
in the likeness of God who "made from one [man]
every nation of men who live on all the face of the
earth" (Acts 17, 26). Love of God and one's neighbor, then, is the first and greatest commandment.
Scripture teaches us that love of God cannot be
separated from love of one's neighbor: "Any other
commandment [is] summed up in this sentence:
You shall love your neighbor as yourself. . . .'
Therefore, love is the fulfilling of the law" (Rom.
13, 9-10; cf. 1 Jn. 4, 20). It goes without saying that
this is a matter of the utmost importance in a world
in which men are coming to rely more and more
on each other, in a world which is drawing closer
together every day.

Furthermore, the Lord Jesus, when praying to
the Father 'that they may all be one . . . even as
we are one' (Jn. 17, 21-22), opened up new horizons closed to human reason by implying that
there is a certain parallel between the union existing among the divine Persons and the union of the
sons of God in truth and love. It follows, then, that
if man is the only creature on earth that God has
wanted for its own sake, man can only fully discover his true self in a sincere giving of himself.[43]

43 Cf. Lk. 17, 33.

Person and Society: Interdependence

25. The social nature of man shows that there is an interdependence between personal betterment and the improvement of society. Insofar as man by his very nature stands completely in need of life in society,[44] he is—as he should be—the beginning, the subject and the object of every social organization. Life in society is not something accessory to man himself; through his dealings with others, through mutual service and through fraternal dialogue, man develops all his talents and becomes able to rise to his destiny.

Among the social ties necessary for man's development, some correspond more immediately to his innermost nature—the family, for instance, and the political community—while others flow from his free choice. Nowadays, for various reasons, mutual relationships and interdependences increase from day to day and give rise to a variety of associations and organizations, both public and private. Socialization, as it is called, is not without its dangers, but it brings with it many advantages for the strengthening and betterment of human qualities and for the protection of human rights.[45]

Missing subjection

While, on the one hand, in fulfilling his calling (even his religious calling) man is greatly helped by life in society, on the other hand it cannot be denied that he is often turned away from good and urged to evil by the social environment in which he lives and in which he has been immersed since the day of his birth. Without doubt, frequent upheavals in the social order are in part the result of economic, political and social tensions. But at a

---

44 Cf. St. Thomas, 1 *Ethica*, Lect. 1.
45 Cf. John XXIII, Encyclical Letter *Mater et Magistra*, May 15, 1961: *A.A.S.* 53 (1961), p. 418; cf. also Pius XI, Encyclical Letter *Quadragesimo anno: A.A.S.* 23 (1931), pp. 222ff.

deeper level they are due to selfishness and pride, two vices which contaminate the atmosphere of society as well. By his very nature man is prone to evil, but whenever he meets a situation where the effects of sin are to be found, he is exposed to further inducements to sin, and these can only be overcome by unflinching efforts under the stimulus of grace.

The Common Good

26.   Because of the closer bonds of human interdependence and their spread over the whole world, we are today witnessing a widening of the role of the common good, which is the sum total of those social conditions which allow people, either as groups or as individuals, to reach their fulfillment more fully and more easily; the whole human race is consequently involved with the whole subject of rights and obligations. Every group must take into account the needs and legitimate aspirations of every other group and still more of the human family as a whole.[46]

At the same time, however, there is a growing awareness of the sublime dignity of the human person who stands above all things and whose rights and duties are universal and inviolable. It is fitting, therefore, that he should have ready access to all that is necessary for living a genuinely human life—for example, food, clothing, housing, the right to freely choose his state of life and set up a family, the right to education, to employment, to his good name, to respect, to proper knowledge, the right to act according to the dictates of conscience, to safeguard his privacy, and to rightful freedom even in matters of religion.

[46] Cf. John XXIII, Encyclical Letter *Mater et Magistra:* *A.A.S.* 53 (1961), p. 417.

The social order and its development must constantly yield to the good of the person, since the order of things must be subordinate to the order of persons and not the other way around, as the Lord suggested when he said that the Sabbath was made for man and not man for the Sabbath.[47] The social order requires constant improvement; it must be founded in truth, built on justice and enlivened by love; it should grow in freedom toward a more humane equilibrium.[48] If these objectives are to be attained, there will first have to be a renewal of attitudes and far-reaching social changes.

The Spirit of God, who with wondrous providence directs the course of time and renews the face of the earth, assists in this development. The ferment of the Gospel has aroused and continues to arouse in the hearts of men an unquenchable thirst for human dignity.

Respect for the Human Person

27. Wishing to discuss topics that are practical and of some urgency, the Council lays stress on respect for the human person. Everyone should look upon his neighbor (without any exception) as another self, bearing in mind above all his life and the means necessary for living it in a dignified way [49] lest he follow the example of the rich man who ignored Lazarus, the poor man. [50]

Today there is an inescapable duty to make ourselves the neighbor of every man, no matter who he is, and to come to his aid in a positive way

---

47 Cf. Mk. 2, 27.
48 Cf. John XXIII, Encyclical Letter *Pacem in terris*: *A.A.S.* 55 (1963) , p. 266.
49 Cf. Jas. 2, 15-16.
50 Cf. Lk. 16, 18-31.

if we meet him, whether he be an aged person abandoned by all, a foreign laborer despised without reason, a refugee, an illegitimate child wrongly suffering for a sin he did not commit, or a starving human being who awakens our conscience by calling to mind the words of Christ: "As you did it to one of the least of these my brethren, you did it to me" (Mt. 25, 40).

The varieties of crime are numerous: all offenses against life, such as murder, genocide, abortion, euthanasia and willful suicide; all violations of the integrity of the human person, such as mutilation, physical and mental torture, and undue psychological pressures; all offenses against human dignity, such as subhuman living conditions, arbitrary imprisonment, deportation, slavery, prostitution, the selling of women and children, and degrading working conditions where men are treated as mere tools for profit rather than as free and responsible persons. All these and similar offenses are criminal, for they poison civilization; furthermore, they debase the perpetrators more than the victims and militate against the honor of the creator.

Respect and Love for Enemies

28.   Those also have a claim on our respect and charity who think and act differently from us in social, political and religious matters. In fact, the more deeply we come to understand their ways of thinking through goodwill and love, the more easily will we be able to undertake dialogue with them.

Love and courtesy of this kind should not, of course, make us indifferent to truth and goodness. Love, in fact, impels the followers of Christ to proclaim to all men the truth which saves. But we must distinguish between the error (which must always be rejected) and the person in error; the latter never loses his dignity as a person even though he flounders amid false or inadequate religious ideas.[51] God alone is the judge and the searcher of hearts; he forbids us to pass judgments on the inner guilt of others.[52]

The teaching of Christ demands that we forgive injury,[53] and the precept of love, which is the commandment of the new law, includes all our enemies: "You have heard that it was said, 'You shall love your neighbor and hate your enemy.' But I say to you, love your enemies, do good to them that hate you, and pray for those who persecute and calumniate you" (Mt. 5, 43-44).

Essential Equality of All Men: Social Justice

29. All men are endowed with a rational soul and created in God's image; they have the same nature and origin and, being redeemed by Christ, they enjoy the same divine calling and destiny. There is here a basic equality between all men and it must be given increasingly greater recognition.

Undoubtedly, not all men are alike as regards physical capacity and intellectual and moral powers. But forms of social or cultural discrimination in basic personal rights on the grounds of sex, race, color, social conditions, language or religion must be curbed and eradicated as incompatible with God's design. It is regrettable that these basic personal rights are still not being respected everywhere, as in the case of women who are denied the chance to freely choose a husband and embark

---

51 Cf. John XXIII, Encyclical Letter *Pacem in terris*: *A.A.S.* 55 (1963), pp. 299-300.

52 Cf. Lk. 6, 37-38; Mt. 7, 1-2; Rom. 2, 1-11; 14, 10-12.

53 Cf. Mt. 5, 43-47.

on a career, or to share in the same educational or cultural benefits available to men.

Furthermore, while there are rightful differences between people, their equal dignity as persons demands that we strive for fairer and more humane conditions. Excessive economic and social disparity between individuals and peoples of the one human race is a source of scandal and militates against social justice, equity and human dignity, as well as social and international peace.

It is up to public and private organizations to be at the service of the dignity and destiny of man. Let them spare no effort to banish every vestige of social and political slavery and to safeguard basic human rights under every political system. Even if it requires considerable time to achieve the desired goal, these organizations should gradually harmonize with spiritual realities, which are the most sublime of all.

Need To Transcend an Individualistic Morality

30.   The pace of change is so far-reaching and rapid nowadays that no one can allow himself to close his eyes to the course of events or indifferently ignore them and wallow in the luxury of a merely individualistic morality. The best way to fulfill one's obligations of justice and love is to contribute to the common good according to one's abilities and the needs of others, even to the point of fostering and helping public and private institutions devoted to bettering the conditions of life. There is a kind of person who boasts of grand and noble sentiments but who lives in practice as if he could not care less about the needs of society. Many in various countries make light of social laws and directives and are not ashamed to resort to fraud

and cheating to avoid paying just taxes and fulfilling other social obligations. Others neglect the norms of social conduct, such as those regulating public hygiene and speed limits, forgetting that they are endangering their own lives and the lives of others by their carelessness.

Let everyone consider it his sacred duty to regard social obligations among man's chief duties today and observe them as such. For the more closely the world comes together, the wider do men's obligations transcend particular groups and gradually extend to the whole world. This will be realized only if individuals and groups practice moral and social virtues and foster them in social living. Then, with the necessary help of divine grace, there will arise a generation of new men, the molders of a new humanity.

Responsibility and Participation

31. To achieve a greater fulfillment of their duties of conscience as individuals toward themselves and the various groups to which they belong, men have to be carefully educated to a higher degree of culture through the employment of the immense resources available today to the human race. Above all we must undertake the training of youth from all social backgrounds if we are to produce the kind of men and women so desperately needed by our age—men and women not only of high culture but of great personality as well.

However, this sense of responsibility will not result unless circumstances are such as to allow man to be conscious of his dignity and to rise to his destiny in the service of God and men. For freedom is often crippled by extreme destitution, just as it can wither in an ivory-tower isolation brought on by overindulgence in the good things of life. It can, however, be strengthened by accepting the inevitable constraints of social life, by undertaking the manifold demands of human coexistence, and by giving service to the community at large.

It is necessary, then, to foster among all the will to play a role in common undertakings. Praise is due to those nations whose policy is to allow the largest possible number of citizens to take part in public affairs in a climate of genuine freedom, although one must always keep in mind the concrete circumstances of each people and the decisiveness required of public authority. Nevertheless, if all citizens are to feel inclined to take part in the activities of the various constituent groups of the social structure, they must find motives in these groups which will attract members and dispose them to serve their fellowmen. One is entitled to think that the future of humanity is in the hands of those men who are capable of providing the generations to come with reasons for life and optimism.

The Word Made Flesh and Human Solidarity

32.   Just as God did not create men to live as individuals but to come together in the formation of social unity, so he "willed to make men holy and save them, not as individuals without any bond or link between them, but rather to make them into a people who might acknowledge him and serve him in holiness".[54] At the outset of salvation history he chose certain men not as individuals but as members of a given community, and he revealed his plan to them, calling them his people (Ex. 3, 7-12) and making a covenant on Mount Sinai with them.[55]

---

[54] Cf. Vatican Council II, *Dogmatic Constitution on the Church,* n. 9: *A.A.S.* 57 (1965), pp. 12–13.
[55] Cf. Exod. 24, 1-8.

This communitarian character was perfected and fulfilled in the work of Jesus Christ, for the Word made flesh willed to share in human fellowship. He was present at the wedding feast at Cana, he visited the house of Zacchaeus, he sat down with publicans and sinners. In revealing the Father's love and man's sublime calling he made use of the most ordinary things of social life, and he illustrated his words with expressions and imagery from everyday life. He sanctified those human ties, particularly family ties, which are the basis of social structures. He willingly observed the laws of his country and chose to lead the life of an ordinary craftsman of his time and country.

In his preaching he clearly outlined an obligation on the part of the sons of God to treat each other as brothers. In his prayer he asked that all his followers should be "one". As the redeemer of all mankind he delivered himself even unto death for the sake of all: "Greater love than this no one has, that one lay down his life for his friends" (Jn. 15, 13). His command to the apostles was to preach the Gospel to all peoples in order that the human race would become the family of God in which love would be the fullness of the law.

As the firstborn of many brethren, Christ established by the gift of his Spirit a new brotherly communion among all who received him in faith and love; this is the communion of his own body, the Church, in which everyone as members one of the other would render mutual service in the measure of the different gifts bestowed on each.

This solidarity must be constantly increased until that day when it will be brought to fulfillment; on that day mankind, saved by grace, will offer perfect glory to God as the family beloved of God and of Christ their brother.

Study-Club Questions

1. What does the biblical "Male and female he created them" tell us of man's existence?

2. What role should the Gospel play in man's contemporary search for human brotherhood?

3. According to the Constitution, "social progress is ambiguous". Where does the ambiguity lie?

4. Discuss the principles of subsidiarity and socialization, pointing out the salient features of each.

5. What is the relation of the individual with his needs and demands to the society in which he lives?

6. The Constitution considers the person always in relation to others. In what way is this consideration trinitarian?

7. The Constitution states that "merely individualistic morality" is difficult to justify in this day and age. Discuss the change in our attitude to personal morality.

8. The demands of love are far more exacting than those of a law could ever be. Discuss.

9. What does the Constitution mean by the common good? What are man's duties in this regard?

10. What examples did Christ give in regard to human fellowship?

CHAPTER III

MAN'S ACTIVITY IN THE UNIVERSE

The Problem

33. Man has always striven to develop his life through his mind and his work; today his efforts have achieved a measure of success, for he has extended and continues to extend his mastery over nearly all spheres of nature, thanks to science and technology. Particularly because of an increase in all kinds of exchange media between nations, the human family is gradually coming to recognize itself as constituting one single community over the whole earth. As a result man now produces by his own enterprise many things which in former times he sought from heavenly powers.

In the face of this immense enterprise now involving the whole human race men are troubled by many questions. What is the meaning and value of this feverish activity? How should all these things be used? To what goal is all this individual and collective enterprise heading? The Church is the guardian of the heritage of the divine Word from which she draws religious and moral principles, but she does not always have a ready answer to every question. Nevertheless, she is eager to associate the light of revelation with the experience of mankind in trying to clarify the course upon which mankind has just entered.

Value of Human Activity

34. Individual and collective activity, that monumental effort of man through the centuries to improve the conditions of human life, presents no problem to believers; considered in itself, it corresponds to the plan of God. Created in God's image, man was commanded to conquer the earth with all it contains and to rule the world in justice and holiness; [56] he was to acknowledge God as the creator of all things and relate himself and the totality of creation to him, so that through the dominion of all things by man the name of God would be majestic throughout the whole earth. [57]

All this also holds true for our daily labor. When men and women provide for themselves and their families in such a way as to be of service to the community as well, they can rightly look upon their work as a prolongation of the work of the creator, a service to their fellowmen, and their personal contribution to the fulfillment in history of the divine plan. [58]

Far from considering the conquests of man's genius and courage as opposed to God's power, as if man set himself up as a rival to the creator, Christians ought to be convinced that the achievements of the human race are a sign of God's greatness and the fulfillment of his ineffable design. With an increase in human power comes a broadening of responsibility on the part of individuals and communities; there is no question, then, of the Christian message inhibiting men from building up the world or making them disinterested in the good of

---

56 Cf. Gen. 1, 26-27; 9, 3; Wis. 9, 3.
57 Cf. Ps. 8, 7. 10.
58 Cf. John XXIII, Encyclical Letter *Pacem in terris*: *A.A.S.* 55 (1963) , p. 297.

their fellowmen; on the contrary, it is an incentive to do these very things.[59]

Regulation of Human Activity

35. Human activity, which proceeds from man, is also ordered to him. When he works, he not only transforms matter and society, but he fulfills himself. He learns, he develops his faculties, and he emerges from and transcends himself. Rightly understood, this kind of growth is more precious than any kind of wealth that can be amassed. It is what a man is, rather than what he has, that counts.[60] Technical progress is of less value than advances toward greater justice, wider brotherhood and a more humane social environment. Technical progress may supply the material for human advance, but it is powerless to actualize it.

Here then is the norm for human activity—to harmonize with the authentic interests of the human race in accordance with God's will and design and to enable men as individuals and as members of society to pursue and fulfill their vocation.

Rightful Autonomy of Earthly Affairs

36. There seems to be some apprehension today that a close association between human activity and religion will endanger the autonomy of man, of organizations and of science. If by the autonomy of earthly affairs is meant the gradual discovery, exploitation and organization of the laws and values of matter and society, then the demand

---

59 Cf. Vatican Council II, *Message to All Mankind,* issued by the fathers at the beginning of the Council, Oct. 20, 1962: *A.A.S.* 54 (1962), p. 823.

60 Cf. Paul VI, *Allocution to the Diplomatic Corps,* Jan. 7, 1965: *A.A.S.* 57 (1965), p. 232.

for autonomy is perfectly in order; it is at once the claim of modern man and the desire of the creator. By the very nature of creation, material being is endowed with its own stability, truth and excellence as well as its own order and laws. Man must respect these as he recognizes the methods proper to every science and technique. Consequently, methodical research in all branches of knowledge, provided it is carried out in a truly scientific manner and does not override moral laws, can never conflict with the faith, because the things of the world and the things of faith derive from the same God.[61] The humble and persevering investigator of the secrets of nature is being led, as it were, by the hand of God in spite of himself, for it is God, the conserver of all things, who made them what they are. We cannot but deplore certain attitudes (not unknown among Christians) deriving from a shortsighted view of the rightful autonomy of science; they have occasioned conflict and controversy and have misled many into opposing faith and science.[62]

However, if by the term "the autonomy of earthly affairs" is meant that material being does not depend on God and that man can use it as if it had no relation to its creator, then the falsity of such a claim will be obvious to anyone who believes in God. Without a creator there can be no creature. In any case, believers, no matter what their religion, have always recognized the voice and the revelation of God in the language of creatures. Besides, once God is forgotten, the creature is lost sight of as well.

---

[61] Cf. Vatican Council I, *Dogmatic Constitution on the Catholic Faith*: Denz. 1785-86 (3004-05).

[62] Cf. Msgr. Pio Paschini, *Vita e opere di Galileo Galilei* (Vatican Press, 1964).

Human Activity Infected by Sin

37. Sacred Scripture teaches mankind what has also been confirmed by man's own experience— namely that the great advantages of human progress are fraught with grave temptations. The hierarchy of values has been disordered, good and evil intermingle, and every man and every group is interested only in its own affairs, not in those of others. As a result the earth has not yet become the scene of true brotherhood; rather man's swelling power at the present time threatens to put an end to the human race itself.

The whole of man's history has been the story of dour combat with the powers of evil, lasting, so our Lord tells us,[63] from the very dawn of history until the last day. Finding himself in the midst of this battlefield, man has to struggle to do what is right, and it is at great cost to himself that he succeeds in achieving his own inner integrity with the help of God's grace. Hence the Church of Christ, trusting in the design of the creator and admitting that progress can contribute to man's true happiness, still feels called upon to echo the words of the apostle: "Be not conformed to this world" (Rom. 12, 2). "World" here means a spirit of vanity and malice whereby human activity, instead of being ordered to the service of God and man, is distorted to an instrument of sin.

To the question of how this unhappy situation can be overcome, Christians reply that all these human activities, which are daily endangered by pride and inordinate self-love, must be purified and perfected by the cross and resurrection of Christ. Redeemed by Christ and made a new creature by the Holy Spirit, man can—indeed must—

---

63 Cf. Mt. 24, 13; 13, 24-30. 36-43.

love the things of God's creation, for he has received them from God and he looks upon them and reveres them as flowing from God's hand. Man thanks his divine benefactor for all these things which he uses and enjoys in a spirit of poverty and freedom; thus he is brought to a true possession of the world, as having nothing, yet possessing everything: [64] "For all things are yours . . . and you are Christ's, and Christ is God's" (1 Cor. 3, 22-23).

Human Activity: Its Fulfillment in the Paschal Mystery

38.   The Word of God, through whom all things were made, became man and dwelt among men; [65] a perfect man, he entered world history, taking that history into himself and recapitulating it.[66] He reveals to us that "God is love" (1 Jn. 4, 8); at the same time he teaches that the fundamental law of human perfection, and consequently of the transformation of the world, is the new commandment of love. He assures those who trust in the charity of God that the way of love is open to all men and that the effort to establish a universal brotherhood will not be in vain.

This love is not something reserved for important matters, but must be exercised above all in the ordinary circumstances of daily life. Christ's example in dying for us sinners [67] teaches us that we must carry the cross which the flesh and the world inflict on the shoulders of all who seek after justice and peace. Constituted Lord by his resurrection and possessing all authority in heaven and on earth,[68] Christ is now at work in the hearts of men

---

64 Cf. 2 Cor. 6, 10.
65 Cf. Jn. 1, 3. 14.
66 Cf. Eph. 1, 10.
67 Cf. Jn. 3, 16; Rom. 5, 8.
68 Cf. Acts 2, 36; Mt. 28, 18.

by the power of his Spirit; not only does he arouse in them a desire for the world to come but he animates, purifies and strengthens the generous aspirations of mankind to make life more humane and to conquer the earth for this purpose. The gifts of the Spirit are manifold. Some are called to testify openly to mankind's yearning for a heavenly home and keep the awareness of it vividly before men's minds; others are called to dedicate themselves to the service of men and in this way to prepare the way for the kingdom of heaven. But the Spirit makes free men of all who are ready to put aside love of self and integrate earthly resources into human life in order to reach out to that future day when mankind itself will become an offering accepted by God. [69]

This is the pledge of hope and the sustenance for the journey which Christ bequeathed to his followers; the sacrament of faith transforms the elements of nature, nurtured by man himself, into his glorious body and blood, the supper of brotherly communion and a foretaste of the heavenly banquet.

A New Earth and a New Heaven

39.   We know neither the moment of the consummation of the earth and of man [70] nor the way the universe will be transformed. The form of this world, distorted by sin, is passing away [71] and we are taught that God is preparing a new dwelling and a new earth in which righteousness dwells,[72] whose happiness will fill and surpass all the desires

---

[69] Cf. Rom. 15, 16.

[70] Cf. Acts 1, 7.

[71] Cf. 1 Cor. 7, 31; cf. also St. Irenaeus, *Adversus haereses* V 36: *P.G.* VIII, 1221.

[72] Cf. 2 Cor. 5, 2; 2 Pet. 3, 13.

of peace arising in the hearts of men.[73] Then with death conquered the sons of God will be raised in Christ, and what was sown in weakness and dishonor will put on the imperishable: [74] charity and its works will remain,[75] and all of creation, which God made for man, will be set free from its bondage to decay.[76]

We have been warned, of course, that it profits man nothing if he gains the whole world and loses or forfeits himself.[77] Far from diminishing our concern to develop this earth, the expectancy of a new earth should spur us on, for it is here that the body of a new human family grows, foreshadowing in some way the age which is to come. Therefore, although we must be careful to clearly distinguish earthly progress from the increase of the kingdom of Christ, such progress is of vital concern to the kingdom of God insofar as it can contribute to the better ordering of human society.[78]

When, according to the command of the Lord and in his Spirit, we have spread on earth the fruits of our nature and our enterprise—human dignity, brotherly communion and freedom—we will find them once again—cleansed this time from the stain of sin, illuminated and transfigured—when Christ presents to his Father an eternal and universal kingdom "of truth and life, a kingdom of holiness and grace, a kingdom of justice, love and peace".[79] Here on earth the kingdom is mysteriously present; when the Lord comes it will enter into its perfection.

---

[73] Cf. 1 Cor. 2, 9; Apoc. 21, 4-5.

[74] Cf. 1 Cor. 15, 42. 53.

[75] Cf. 1 Cor. 13, 8; 3, 14.

[76] Cf. Rom. 8, 19-21.

[77] Cf. Lk. 9, 25.

[78] Cf. Pius XI, Encyclical Letter *Quadragesimo anno: A.A.S.* 23 (1931), p. 207.

[79] Cf. *Preface for the Feast of Christ the King.*

Study-Club Questions

1. Some people believe that the Christian concern for the eternal can lead only to neglect of the temporal. Discuss.

2. In what sense is man's work in the world basically creative?

3. What does the Constitution mean when it says: "Human activity takes its significance, its measure and its value from the human person"?

4. Why did Christians of former centuries fear science and its developments? Does this fear exist today?

5. In what way can progress be a source of temptation?

6. How does the Gospel open man's eyes to the illness present in society and lead him to the Spirit?

7. What is meant in the Constitution by the expression "the world"?

8. The Constitution states that through his resurrection "Christ is now at work in the hearts of men by the power of his Spirit". Discuss.

9. Inasmuch as the Christian lives in the present in anticipation of the kingdom of God, his hope is eschatological. What does this mean?

10. How is human activity fulfilled in the paschal mystery?

CHAPTER IV

THE ROLE OF THE CHURCH IN THE MODERN WORLD

Mutual Relationship of Church and World

40.   All we have said up to now about the dignity of the human person, the community of mankind and the deep significance of human activity provides a basis for discussing the relationship between the Church and the world and the dialogue between them.[80] In the light of what it has already declared about the mystery of the Church, the Council now intends to consider the presence of the Church in the world and her life and activity there.

Proceeding from the love of the eternal Father,[81] the Church was founded by Christ in time and gathered into one by the Holy Spirit; [82] her end is saving and eschatological and can only be fully attained in the next life. She is now present here on earth and is composed of men; they, the members of the earthly city, are called to form the family of the children of God even in this present history of mankind and to increase it continually

---

80 Cf. Paul VI, Encyclical Letter *Ecclesiam suam*: *A.A.S.* 56 (1964), pp. 637-59.
81 Cf. Tit. 3, 4: "love of mankind".
82 Cf. Eph. 1, 3; 5, 6. 13-14. 23.

until the Lord comes. Made one in view of heavenly benefits and enriched by them, this family has been "constituted and organized as a society in the present world" [83] by Christ and "provided with means adapted to its visible and social union".[84] Thus the Church, at once "a visible organization and a spiritual community",[85] travels the same journey as all mankind and shares the same earthly lot with the world; she is to be a leaven and, as it were, the soul of human society in its renewal by Christ [86] and transformation into the family of God.

That the earthly and the heavenly city penetrate one another is a fact open only to the eyes of faith; moreover, it will remain the mystery of human history which will be harassed by sin until the perfect revelation of the splendor of the sons of God. In pursuing her own salvific purpose, the Church not only communicates divine life to men but in a certain sense she also casts the reflected light of that divine life over all the earth, notably in the way she heals and elevates the dignity of the human person, consolidates society and endows the daily activity of men with a deeper sense and meaning. The Church, then, believes she can contribute much to humanizing the family of man and its history through each of her members and her community as a whole.

Furthermore, the Catholic Church holds in high esteem what other Christian Churches and ecclesial communities have contributed and are contributing cooperatively to the realization of this

---

[83] Cf. Vatican Council II, *Dogmatic Constitution on the Church*, n. 8: *A.A.S.* 57 (1965), p. 12.

[84] Cf. *ibid.*, n. 9: *A.A.S.* 57 (1965), p. 14; also cf. *ibid.*, n. 8, p. 11.

[85] Cf. *ibid.*, n. 8: *A.A.S.* 57 (1965), p. 11.

[86] Cf. *ibid.*, n. 38: *A.A.S.* 57 (1965), p. 43, with footnote 120.

aim. Similarly, she is convinced that there is a considerable and varied help that she can receive from the world in the preparation of the Gospel, both from individuals and from society as a whole by their talents and activity. The Council will now outline some general principles for the proper fostering of mutual exchange and assistance in matters which are in some way common to the Church and the world.

What the Church Offers to All Men

41.   Modern man is in a process of fuller personality development and a growing discovery and affirmation of his own rights. But the Church is entrusted with the task of opening up to man the mystery of God who is the last end of man; in doing so she opens up to him the innermost truth about himself. The Church knows well that God alone, whom she serves, can satisfy the deepest cravings of the human heart, for the world and what it has to offer can never fully give it perfect contentment. She also realizes that man is continually being aroused by the Spirit of God and that he will never be utterly indifferent to religion—a fact confirmed by the experience of ages past and plentiful evidence of the present day. For man will ever be anxious to know, if only in a vague way, what is the meaning of his life, his activity and his death. The most perfect answer to these questionings is to be found in God alone, who created man in his own image and redeemed him from sin, and this answer is given in the revelation in Christ his Son who became man. Whoever follows Christ, the perfect man, becomes himself more a man.

Relying on this faith the Church can raise the dignity of human nature above all fluctuating opinions which, for example, would unduly despise or idolize the human body. There is no human law as powerful to safeguard the personal dignity and freedom of man as the Gospel which Christ entrusted to the Church; for the Gospel announces and proclaims the freedom of the sons of God; it rejects all bondage resulting from sin,[87] it scrupulously respects the dignity and freedom of choice of conscience, it never ceases to encourage the employment of human talents in the service of God and man, and, finally, it commends everyone to the charity of all.[88] This is nothing other than the basic law of the Christian scheme of things. God who is creator is also redeemer; the same God who is Lord of salvation history is Lord of human history as well. This does not mean that the autonomy of the creature, of man in particular, is suppressed; on the contrary, in the divine order of things all this redounds to the restoration and consolidation of this autonomy.

In virtue of the Gospel entrusted to her, the Church proclaims the rights of man; moreover, she acknowledges and holds in high esteem the dynamic approach of today which is fostering these rights all over the world. But this approach needs to be animated by the spirit of the Gospel and preserved from all traces of false autonomy. For there is a temptation to feel that our personal rights are only fully maintained when we are exempt from every restriction of divine law. However, this way leads to the extinction of human dignity, not its preservation.

What the Church Offers to Society

42.   The union of the family of man is greatly

---

87 Cf. Rom. 8, 14-17.
88 Cf. Mt. 22, 39.

consolidated and perfected by the unity which Christ established among the sons of God.[89] Christ did not bequeath to the Church a mission in the political, economic or social order: the end he assigned to her was a religious one.[90] But this religious mission can be the source of commitment, direction and vigor to establish and consolidate the community of men according to the law of God. In fact, the Church is able—indeed she is obliged if times and circumstances require it—to initiate action for the benefit of all men, especially of those in need, such as works of charity and similar undertakings.

Moreover, the Church acknowledges the good to be found in the social dynamism of today, particularly progress toward unity, healthy socialization and civil and economic cooperation. The encouragement of unity is in harmony with the deepest nature of the Church's mission, for she "is in the nature of a sacrament—a sign and instrument —of communion with God and of unity among all men".[91] She shows the world that social and exterior union results from a union of hearts and minds, from the faith and love by which her own indissoluble unity has been founded in the Holy

---

[89] Cf. Vatican Council II, *Dogmatic Constitution on the Church,* n. 9: *A.A.S.* 57 (1965), pp. 12-14.

[90] Cf. Pius XII, *Allocution to Historians and Artists,* March 9, 1956: *A.A.S.* 48 (1965), p. 212: "Her divine founder, Jesus Christ, has not given her any mandate or fixed any end of the cultural order. The goal which Christ assigns to her is strictly religious. . . . The Church must lead men to God in order that they may be given over to him without reserve. . . . The Church can never lose sight of the strictly religious, supernatural goal. The meaning of all her activities, down to the last canon of her Code, can only cooperate directly or indirectly in this goal."

[91] Cf. Vatican Council II, *Dogmatic Constitution on the Church,* n. 1: *A.A.S.* 57 (1965), p. 5.

Spirit. The impact which the Church can have on modern society amounts to an effective living of faith and love, not to any external power exercised by purely human means.

By her nature and mission the Church is universal in that she is not committed to any one culture or to any political, economic or social system. Hence she can have a great unifying effect on the various communities of men and nations, provided they have trust in the Church and guarantee her freedom to carry out her mission. With this in view the Church calls upon her members and upon all men to put aside in the family spirit of the children of God all conflict between nations and races and to consolidate legitimate human organizations.

Whatever truth, goodness and justice is to be found in past or present human institutions is held in high esteem by the Council. In addition, the Council declares that the Church is anxious to help and foster these institutions insofar as it is possible and compatible with her mission. The Church desires nothing more ardently than to develop herself untrammeled in the service of all men under any regime which recognizes the basic rights of the person and the family and the needs of the common good.

What the Church Offers to Human Activity through Her Members

43.   The Council exhorts Christians, as citizens of both cities, to perform their duties faithfully in the spirit of the Gospel. It is a mistake to think that, because we have here no lasting city, but seek the city which is to come,[92] we are entitled to shirk our earthly responsibilities; this is to forget that by

---

[92] Cf. Heb. 13, 14.

our faith we are bound all the more to fulfill these responsibilities according to the vocation of each one.[93] But we are no less mistaken to think that we may immerse ourselves in earthly activities as if these latter were utterly foreign to religion and religion were nothing more than the fulfillment of acts of worship and the observance of a few moral obligations. One of the gravest errors of our time is the dichotomy between the faith which many profess and the practice of their daily lives. As far back as the Old Testament the prophets vehemently denounced this scandal [94] and in the New Testament Christ himself with greater force threatened it with severe punishment.[95] Therefore, let there be no such pernicious opposition between professional and social activity and religious life. The Christian who shirks his temporal duties shirks his duties toward his neighbor, neglects God himself and endangers his eternal salvation. Let Christians follow the example of Christ who worked as a craftsman; let them be proud of the opportunity to carry out their earthly activity in such a way as to integrate human, domestic, professional, scientific and technical enterprises with religious values, because under the direction of religion all things are ordered to the glory of God.

It is to the laity, though not exclusively to them, that secular duties and activity properly belong. When, therefore, as citizens of the world, they are engaged either in individual or collective activity, they will not merely observe the laws proper to each discipline but will also strive to become proficient in that field. They will gladly cooperate with others working toward the same objectives.

---

93 Cf. 2 Thes. 3, 6-13; Eph. 4, 28.
94 Cf. Is. 58, 1-12.
95 Cf. Mt. 23, 3-23; Mk. 7, 10-13.

Let them be aware of what their faith demands of them in these matters and derive strength from it; let them not hesitate to take the initiative at the opportune moment and put their findings into effect. It is their task to cultivate a properly informed conscience and to impress the divine law on the affairs of the earthly city. For guidance and spiritual strength let them turn to the clergy, but let them realize that their pastors will not always be so expert as to have a ready answer to every problem (even every grave problem) that arises. This is not the role of the clergy; it is rather up to the laymen to shoulder their responsibilities under the guidance of Christian wisdom and with eager attention to the teaching of the magisterium.[96]

It may happen that the laity's Christian vision will suggest a certain solution in some given situation. As often happens, there will be some of the faithful who with no less sincerity will see the problem quite differently; this is as it should be. Now if one or another of the proposed solutions is too easily associated with the message of the Gospel, they ought to remember that in those cases no one is permitted to identify the authority of the Church exclusively with his own opinion. Let them then try to guide each other by sincere dialogue in a spirit of mutual charity and with anxious interest above all in the common good.

The laity are called to participate actively in the whole life of the Church; not only are they to animate the world with the spirit of Christianity, but they are to be witnesses to Christ in all circumstances and at the very heart of the community of mankind.

To the bishops has been committed the task of

---

[96] Cf. John XXIII, Encyclical Letter *Mater et Magistra*: *A.A.S.* 53 (1961), pp. 456-57; also cf. *ibid.*, pp. 407, 410-11.

directing the Church of God; together with the priests they are to preach the message of Christ in such a way that the light of the Gospel will impregnate all activities of the faithful. Let all pastors of souls be careful to build up by their daily behavior and concern [97] an image of the Church capable of impressing men with the power and truth of the Christian message. By their words and example and in union with religious and with the faithful, let them show that the Church with all her gifts is, by her presence alone, an inexhaustible font of all those resources of which the modern world stands in such dire need. Let them prepare themselves by careful study to meet and play their part in dialogue with the world and with men of all shades of opinion; let them have in their hearts above all these words of the Council: "Since the human race today is tending more and more toward civil, economic and social unity, it is all the more necessary that priests should unite their efforts and combine their resources under the leadership of the bishops and the supreme pontiff and thus eliminate division and dissension in every shape or form, so that all mankind may be led into the unity of the family of God." [98]

By the power of the Holy Spirit, the Church is the faithful spouse of the Lord and will never fail to be a sign of salvation in the world, but she is by no means unaware that down through the centuries there have been among her members,[99] both clerical and lay, some who were disloyal to the Spirit of God. Today as well the Church is not blind to the discrepancy between the message she proclaims

---

[97] Cf. Vatican Council II, *Dogmatic Constitution on the Church*, n. 28: *A.A.S.* 57 (1965), p. 35.

[98] Cf. *ibid.*, n. 28, pp. 35-36.

[99] Cf. St. Ambrose, *De virginitate*, n. 48: *M.L.* 16, 278.

and the human weakness of those to whom the Gospel has been entrusted. Whatever is history's judgment on these shortcomings, we cannot ignore them; rather, we must combat them earnestly lest they hinder the spread of the Gospel. The Church also realizes how greatly she needs the maturing influences of centuries of past experience in order to work out her relationship to the world. Guided by the Holy Spirit the Church ceaselessly "exhorts her children to purification and renewal so that the sign of Christ may shine more brightly over the face of the Church".[100]

What the Church Receives from the Modern World

44.   Just as it is in the world's interest to acknowledge the Church as a social reality and a driving force in history, so too the Church is not unaware how much she has profited from the history and development of mankind. She has profited from the experience of past ages, from the progress of the sciences and from the riches hidden in various cultures through which greater light is thrown on the nature of man and new avenues to truth are opened up. The Church learned early in her history to express the Christian message in the concepts and language of different peoples and tried to clarify it in the light of the wisdom of their philosophers; it was an attempt to adapt the Gospel to the understanding of all men and the requirements of the learned, insofar as this could be done. Indeed, this kind of adaptation and preaching of the revealed Word must ever be the law of all evangelization. In this way it is possible to create in every

---

[100] Cf. Vatican Council II, *Dogmatic Constitution on the Church*, n. 15: *A.A.S.* 57 (1965), p. 20.

country the possibility of expressing the message of Christ in suitable terms and to foster vital contact and exchange between the Church and different cultures.[101] In these days of such rapid change when thought patterns differ so widely, the Church needs to step up this exchange by calling upon the help of people who are living in the world, who are expert in its organizations and its forms of training, and who understand its mentality in the case of believers and non-believers alike. It is the task of the whole People of God, particularly of its pastors and theologians, to listen to and distinguish the many voices of our times and to interpret them in the light of the divine Word in order that the revealed truth may be more deeply penetrated, better understood and more suitably presented.

The Church has a visible social structure which is a sign of her unity in Christ; as such she can be enriched, and she is being enriched, by the evolution of social life—not as if something were missing in the constitution which Christ gave the Church, but in order to understand this constitution more deeply, express it better and adapt it more successfully to our times. The Church is happy to feel that with regard to both the community she forms and each of her members, she is assisted in various ways by men of all classes and conditions. Whoever contributes to the development of the community of mankind on the level of family, culture, economic and social life, and national and international politics, according to the plan of God, is also contributing in no small way to the community of the Church. The Church herself also recognizes that she has benefited and is still benefiting from the opposition of her enemies and persecutors.[102]

---

101 Cf. *ibid.*, n. 13, p. 17.
102 Cf. Justin, *Dialogus cum Tryphone,* Ch. 110: *M.G.* 6, 729

Christ, Alpha and Omega

45.   Whether she aids the world or whether she benefits from it, the Church has but one sole purpose—that the kingdom of God may come and the salvation of the human race may be accomplished. Every benefit the People of God can confer on mankind during its earthly pilgrimage is rooted in the Church's being "the universal sacrament of salvation",[103] at once manifesting and actualizing the mystery of God's love for men.

The Word of God, through whom all things were made, was made flesh so that as a perfect man he could save all men and recapitulate all things in himself. The Lord is the goal of human history, the focal point of the desires of history and civilization, the center of mankind, the joy of all hearts and the fulfillment of all aspirations.[104] It is he whom the Father raised from the dead, exalted and placed at his right hand, constituting him judge of the living and the dead. Animated and drawn together in his Spirit we press onward on our journey toward the consummation of history which fully corresponds to the plan of his love: ". . . to reestablish all things in Christ, both those in the heavens and those on the earth" (Eph. 1, 10).

(ed. Otto, 1897), pp. 391-93: ". . . but the greater the number of persecutions which are inflicted upon us, so much the greater the number of other men who become devout believers through the name of Jesus." Cf. Tertullian, *Apologeticus*, Ch. 50, 13: *Corpus Christi,* ser. lat. I, p. 171: "Every time you mow us down like grass, we increase in number: the blood of Christians is a seed." Cf. Vatican Council II, *Dogmatic Constitution on the Church,* n. 9: *A.A.S.* 57 (1965), p. 14.

103 Cf. Vatican Council II, *Dogmatic Constitution on the Church,* n. 15: *A.A.S.* 57 (1965), p. 20.

104 Cf. Paul VI, Allocution of Feb. 3, 1965.

The Lord himself said: "Behold, I come quickly! And my reward is with me, to render to each one according to his works. I am the Alpha and the Omega, the first and the last, the beginning and the end" (Apoc. 22, 12-13).

Study-Club Questions

1. What has caused the modern Church to reconsider her sense of mission to the world?

2. In what ways must the Church reevaluate her mission? What new directions is it taking or is it likely to take? What difficulties does it present?

3. How does the Church reveal to man "the innermost truth about himself"?

4. How do you explain the Spirit's presence in human life prior to the preaching of the Gospel?

5. Why is there a continuing need to preach the Gospel?

6. The Church is in dialogue with the world. Discuss.

7. How must a Christian reconcile his eternal and supernatural calling and his present temporal tasks?

8. Why is it necessary for the Church to have a visible social structure? Can she ever change this structure? If so, how?

9. "The Church herself also recognizes that she has benefited and is still benefiting from the opposition of her enemies and persecutors." Explain.

10. How is the Church preparing for the coming of the kingdom of Christ and his second coming in the present day?

PART II

Preface

46. Having set forth the dignity of the human person and his individual and social role in the universe, the Council now draws the attention of men, in the light of the Gospel and of human experience, to the consideration of some problems of special urgency affecting the human race at the present time.

Of the many problems which excite general interest today it may be helpful to concentrate on the following: marriage and the family, culture, economic and social life, politics, the solidarity of peoples and peace. We must seek light for each of these problems from the principles which Christ has given us; in this way the faithful will receive guidance and all men will be enlightened in their search for solutions to such numerous and complicated problems.

CHAPTER I

THE DIGNITY OF MARRIAGE AND THE FAMILY

Marriage and the Family in the Modern World

47. The well-being of the individual person as well as of human and Christian society is closely bound up with the healthy state of conjugal and family life. Hence Christians today are overjoyed, as are all who esteem conjugal and family life highly, to witness the various ways in which progress is being made in fostering those partnerships of love and in encouraging reverence for human life. There also has been progress in services available to married people and parents for fulfilling their lofty calling; even greater benefits are to be expected and efforts are being made to bring them about.

However, this happy picture of the dignity of these partnerships is not reflected everywhere, but is overshadowed by polygamy, the plague of divorce, so-called free love, and similar evils; furthermore, married love is far too often profaned by selfishness, hedonism and illicit contraceptive practices. In addition, the economic, social, psychological and civil climate of today has a severely disturbing effect on family life. There are also the serious and alarming problems arising in many parts of the world as a result of the population explosion. On all of these counts an anguish of conscience is being generated. And yet the strength and vigor of the institutions of marriage and the family shine forth time and again, for despite the hardships flowing from the profoundly changing conditions of society today, the true nature of marriage and the family is revealed in one way or another.

It is for these reasons that the Council intends to present certain key points of the Church's teaching in a clearer light; it hopes thereby to guide and encourage Christians and all men who are trying to preserve and to foster the dignity and supremely sacred value of the married state.

Sanctity of Marriage and the Family

48. The intimate partnership of life and love which constitutes the married state has been established by the creator and endowed by him with its own proper laws; it is rooted in the conjugal covenant of irrevocable personal consent. It is an institution confirmed by the divine law and receiving its stability, even in the eyes of society, from the human act by which the spouses mutually surrender themselves to each other; for the good of the partners, of the children, and of society this sacred bond no longer depends on human decision alone. For God himself is the author of marriage and has endowed it with various benefits and with various ends in view; [105] all of these have a very important bearing on the continuation of the human race, on the personal development and eternal destiny of every member of the family, and on the dignity,

---

[105] Cf. St. Augustine, *De bono coniugii*: *P.L.* 40, 375-76, 394; St. Thomas, *Summa Theologica: Suppl. Quaest.* 49, art. 3 ad 1; St. Thomas, *Decretum pro Armenis*: *Denz.-Schön.* 1327; Pius XI, Encyclical Letter *Casti connubii*: *A.A.S.* 22 (1930), pp. 547-48 (*Denz.-Schön.* 3703-14).

stability, peace and prosperity of the family and of the whole human race. By its very nature the institution of marriage and married love is ordered to the procreation and education of the offspring and it is in them that it finds its crowning glory. Thus the man and woman, who "are no longer two, but one flesh" (Mt. 19, 6), give mutual help and service to each other by their marriage partnership, through which they become conscious of their unity and experience it more deeply with each passing day. The intimate union of marriage, as a mutual giving of two persons, and the good of the children demand total fidelity from the spouses and require an unbreakable unity between them.[106]

Christ our Lord has abundantly blessed this many-faceted love which is rich in its various features, coming as it does from the spring of divine love and modeled on Christ's own union with the Church. Just as of old God encountered his people with a covenant of love and fidelity,[107] so our Savior, the spouse of the Church,[108] now encounters Christian spouses through the sacrament of marriage. He abides with them in order that by their mutual self-giving spouses will love each other with enduring fidelity, as he loved the Church and delivered himself for her.[109] Authentic married love is caught up into divine love and is directed and enriched by the redemptive power of Christ and the salvific action of the Church, with the result that the spouses are effectively led to God and are

---

[106] Cf. Pius XI, Encyclical Letter *Casti connubii*: *A.A.S.* 22 (1930), pp. 546-47 (Denz.-Schön. 3706).

[107] Cf. Hos. 2; Jer. 3, 6-13; Ezech. 16; 23; Is. 54.

[108] Cf. Mt. 9, 15; Mk. 2, 19-20; Lk. 5, 34-35; Jn. 3, 29. Cf. also 2 Cor. 11, 2; Eph. 5, 27; Apoc. 19, 7-8; 21, 2. 9.

[109] Cf. Eph. 5, 25.

helped and strengthened in their lofty role as fathers and mothers.[110] Spouses, therefore, are fortified and, as it were, consecrated for the duties and dignity of their state by a special sacrament;[111] fulfilling their conjugal and family role by virtue of this sacrament, spouses are penetrated with the spirit of Christ and their whole life is suffused by faith, hope and charity; thus they increasingly further their own perfection and their mutual sanctification, and together they render glory to God.

Inspired by the example and family prayer of their parents, children—and, in fact, everyone living under the family roof—will more easily set out upon the path of a truly human training, of salvation and of holiness. As for the spouses, when they are given the dignity and role of fatherhood and motherhood, they will eagerly carry out their duties of education, especially religious education, which primarily devolves on them.

As living members of the family, children contribute in their own way to the sanctification of their parents. With sentiments of gratitude, affection and trust, they will repay their parents for the benefits given to them and will come to their assistance as devoted children in times of hardship and in the loneliness of old age. Widowhood, accepted courageously as a continuation of the calling to marriage, will be honored by all.[112] Families will generously share their spiritual treasures with other families. The Christian family springs from marriage,[113] which is an image and a sharing in the

---

110 Cf. Vatican Council II, *Dogmatic Constitution on the Church: A.A.S.* 57 (1965), pp. 15-16, 40-41, 47.

111 Cf. Pius XI, Encyclical Letter *Casti connubii: A.A.S.* 22 (1930), p. 583.

112 Cf. 1 Tim. 5, 3.

113 Cf. Eph. 5, 32.

partnership of love between Christ and the Church; it will show forth to all men Christ's living presence in the world and the authentic nature of the Church by the love and generous fruitfulness of the spouse, by their unity and fidelity, and by the loving way in which all members of the family cooperate with each other.

Married Love

49. On several occasions the Word of God invites the betrothed to nourish and foster their betrothal with chaste love, and likewise spouses their marriage.[114] Many of our contemporaries also have a high regard for true love between husband and wife as it manifests itself in the worthy customs of various times and peoples. Married love is an eminently human love because it involves affection between two persons that is rooted in the will and it embraces the good of the whole person; it can enrich the sentiments of the spirit and their physical expression with a unique dignity and ennoble them as the special elements and signs of the friendship proper to marriage. The Lord, wishing to bestow special gifts of grace and divine love on marriage, has restored, perfected and elevated it. Such a love, bringing together the human and the divine, leads the partners to a free and mutual giving of self, experienced in tenderness and action, and permeates their whole lives; [115] besides, this love is actually developed and increases by its exercise. This is a far cry from mere erotic attraction,

---

114 Cf. Gen. 2, 22-24; Prov. 5, 15-20; 31, 10-31; Tob. 8, 4-8; Cant. 1, 2-3. 16; 4, 16—5, 1; 7, 8-14; 1 Cor. 7, 3-6; Eph. 5, 25-33.
115 Cf. Pius XI, Encyclical Letter *Casti connubii*: *A.A.S.* 22 (1930), pp. 547-48 (*Denz.-Schön.* 3707).

which is pursued in selfishness and soon fades away in wretchedness.

Married love is uniquely expressed and perfected by the exercise of the acts proper to marriage. Hence the acts in marriage, by which the intimate and chaste union of the spouses takes place, are noble and honorable; the truly human performance of these acts fosters the self-giving they signify and enriches the spouses in joy and gratitude. Endorsed by mutual fidelity and, above all, consecrated by Christ's sacrament, this love abides faithfully in mind and body during times of prosperity and adversity and hence excludes both adultery and divorce. The unity of marriage, distinctly recognized by our Lord, is made clear in the equal personal dignity which must be accorded to man and wife in mutual and unreserved affection. Outstanding courage is required for the constant fulfillment of the duties of this Christian calling. Spouses, therefore, will need grace to lead a holy life; they will eagerly practice a love that is firm, generous and prompt to sacrifice, and they will ask for it in their prayers.

Authentic married love will be held in high esteem and healthy public opinion will be quick to recognize it if Christian spouses give outstanding witness to faithfulness and harmony in their love, if they are conspicuous in their concern for the education of their children, and if they play their part in a much needed cultural, psychological and social renewal in matters of marriage and the family. It is imperative to give suitable and timely instruction to young people, particularly within their own families, about the dignity of married love, its role and its exercise; in this way they will be able to engage in honorable courtship and enter upon marriages of their own.

The Fruitfulness of Marriage

50. Marriage and married love are by nature ordered to the procreation and education of children. Indeed, children are the supreme gift of marriage and greatly contribute to the good of the parents themselves. God himself said: "It is not good that the man is alone" (Gen. 2, 18), and "from the beginning [he] made them male and female" (Mt. 19, 4); wishing to associate them in a special way with his own creative work, God blessed man and woman with the words: "Be fruitful and multiply" (Gen. 1, 28). Without intending to underestimate the other ends of marriage, it must be said that true conjugal love and the whole structure of family life which results from it are directed to disposing the spouses to cooperate valiantly with the love of the creator and Savior who through them will increase and enrich his family with each passing day.

Married couples should regard it as their proper mission to transmit human life and to educate their children; they should realize that they are thereby cooperating with the love of God the creator and are, in a certain sense, its interpreters. This involves the fulfillment of their role with a sense of human and Christian responsibility and the formation of correct judgments through docile respect for God and common reflection and effort; it also involves a consideration of their own good and the good of their children already born or yet to come, an ability to read the signs of the times and of their own situation on the material and spiritual level, and, finally, an estimation of the good of the family, society and the Church. It is the married couple themselves who must ultimately make these judgments before God. Married people should realize that in their behavior they may not simply follow their own fancy but must be ruled by conscience—

and conscience should be conformed to the law of God in the light of the magisterium of the Church which is the authentic interpreter of divine law. For the divine law throws light on the meaning of married love, protects it and leads it to truly human fulfillment. Whenever Christian spouses in a spirit of sacrifice and trust in divine providence [116] carry out their duties of procreation with a generous, human and Christian sense of responsibility, they glorify the creator and perfect themselves in Christ. Among the married couples who thus fulfill their God-given mission, special mention should be made of those who after prudent reflection and common decision courageously undertake the proper upbringing of a larger number of children.[117]

But marriage is not merely for the procreation of children; its nature as an indissoluble compact between two people and the good of the children demand that the mutual love of the partners be properly shown and that it grow and mature. Even in cases where, despite the intense desire of the spouses, there are no children, marriage still retains its character of being the community and communion of their entire life and preserves its value and indissolubility.

Married Love and Respect for Human Life

51. The Council realizes that in modern life married people are often hindered by certain situations from working out their married love harmoniously and that they can sometimes find themselves in a position where the number of children cannot be increased, at least for the time be-

---

[116] Cf. 1 Cor. 7, 5.
[117] Cf. Pius XII, Address *Tra le visite,* Jan. 20, 1958: *A.A.S.* 50 (1958), p. 91.

ing; in cases like these it is quite difficult to preserve the practice of faithful love and the complete intimacy of their lives. But where the intimacy of married life is broken, it often happens that faithfulness is imperiled and the good of the children suffers; then the education of the children and the courage to accept more children are both endangered.

Some of the proposed solutions to these problems are shameful; some people have even not hesitated to suggest murder. The Church wishes to emphasize that there can be no conflict between the divine laws governing the transmission of life and the fostering of authentic married love.

God, the Lord of life, has entrusted to men the noble mission of safeguarding life, and men must carry it out in a manner worthy of them. Life must be protected with the utmost care from the moment of conception: abortion and infanticide are abominable crimes. The sexual characteristics of man and the human faculty of reproduction wondrously surpass the endowments of lower forms of life; therefore the acts proper to married life are to be ordered according to authentic human dignity and must be honored with the greatest reverence. When it is a question of harmonizing married love with the responsible transmission of life, it is not enough to take only the good intention and the evaluation of motives into account; objective criteria must be used, criteria drawn from the nature of the human person and human action, criteria which respect the total meaning of mutual self-giving and human procreation in the context of true love. All this is possible only if the virtue of married chastity is seriously practiced. In questions of birth regulation the sons of the Church, faithful to these principles, are forbidden to use methods disapproved by the magisterium in its interpretation of the divine law.[118]

Let all be convinced that human life and its transmission are realities whose meaning is not limited by the horizons of this life only; their true evaluation and full meaning can only be understood in reference to man's eternal destiny.

Promotion of Marriage and the Family: A Duty for All

52. The family is, in a sense, a school for human enrichment. But if it is to achieve the full flowering of its life and mission, the married couple must practice an affectionate sharing of thought and common reflection together with their eager cooperation as parents in the children's upbringing. The active presence of the father is very important for their training; the mother, too, has a central role in the home, for the children, especially the younger children, depend on her considerably; this role must be safeguarded without, however, underrating woman's legitimate social advancement. The education of children should be such that when they grow up they will be able to follow their vocation, including a religious vocation, and choose their state of life with full con-

---

118 Cf. Pius XI, Encyclical Letter *Casti connubii*: *A.A.S.* 22 (1930), pp. 559-61 (*Denz.-Schön.* 3716-18); Pius XII, *Allocution to Obstetricians*, Oct. 29, 1951: *A.A.S.* 43 (1951), pp. 835-54; Paul VI, *Allocution to Cardinals,* June 23, 1964: *A.A.S.* (1964), p. 581-89. Certain questions which need further and more careful investigation have been handed over, at the command of the supreme pontiff, to a commission for the study of population, family and births in order that, after it fulfills its function, the supreme pontiff may pass judgment. With the teaching of the magisterium in this state, this holy synod does not intend to propose concrete solutions immediately.

sciousness of responsibility; if they marry they should be capable of setting up a family in favorable moral, social and economic circumstances. It is the duty of parents and teachers to guide young people with prudent advice in the establishment of a family; their interest should make young people listen to them eagerly and they should beware of exercising any undue influence, directly or indirectly, to force them into marriage or compel them in their choice of partner.

The family is the place where different generations come together and help one another to grow wiser and harmonize the rights of individuals with other demands of social life; as such it constitutes the basis of society. Therefore, everyone who exercises an influence in the community and in social groups should devote himself effectively to the welfare of marriage and the family. Civil authority should consider it a sacred duty to acknowledge the true nature of marriage and the family, to protect and foster them, to safeguard public morality and to promote domestic prosperity. The rights of parents to procreate and educate children in the family must be safeguarded. There should also be welfare legislation and provision made for the protection and assistance of those who unfortunately have been deprived of the benefits of family life.

Christians, making full use of the times in which we live and carefully distinguishing the everlasting from the changeable, should actively strive to promote the values of marriage and the family. This can be done by the witness of their own lives and by concerted action along with all men of goodwill; in this way they will overcome obstacles and make provision for the requirements and the advantages of the family arising at the present day. To this end the Christian instincts of the faithful, the right moral conscience of man and the wisdom and skill of persons versed in the sacred sciences will have much to contribute.[119]

Experts in other sciences, particularly biology, medicine, social science and psychology, can be of service to the welfare of marriage and the family and the peace of mind of people, if by pooling their efforts they try to clarify thoroughly the various conditions favoring the proper regulation of births.

It devolves on priests to be properly trained to deal with family matters and to nurture the vocation of married people in their married and family life by different pastoral means, by the preaching of the Word of God, by liturgy and by other spiritual assistance. They should strengthen them sympathetically and patiently in their difficulties and comfort them in charity with a view to the formation of truly radiant families.

Various organizations, especially family associations, should attempt by their programs of instruction and activity to strengthen young people, especially young married people, and to prepare them for family, social and apostolic life.

Let married people themselves, who are created in the image of the living God and constituted in an authentic personal dignity, be united together in equal affection, agreement of mind and mutual holiness.[120] Thus, in the footsteps of Christ, the principle of life,[121] they will bear witness by their faithful love, in the joys and sacrifices of their calling, to that mystery of love which the Lord revealed to the world by his death and resurrection.[122]

---

[119] Cf. Eph. 5, 16; Col. 4, 5.
[120] Cf. *Sacramentarium Gregorianum*: *P.L.* 78, 262.
[121] Cf. Rom. 5, 15. 18; 6, 5-11; Gal. 2, 20.
[122] Cf. Eph. 5, 25-27.

Study-Club Questions

1. In this Constitution the Church lays particular stress on the role of conjugal love, highlighting its positive aspects. In what respect does this differ from past considerations on marriage?

2. The relationship between family life and the well-being of individuals and society is reciprocal. How does society at large depend upon the health of the family and its sound development? How are family members dependent upon society? What elements of family life are common to the life of the personal members and society?

3. Regarding responsible parenthood, the Constitution asserts: "Married couples themselves . . . must ultimately make these judgments before God." Upon what criteria are these judgments to be made?

4. What is the relation between personal motivations and objective norms? How do they affect each other?

5. Christian marriage is personal at the same time that it is sacramental. Discuss.

6. What does the Constitution mean when it states: "Marriage and married love are by nature ordered to the procreation and education of children"? How do you compare this with what it says of conjugal love?

7. Christian marriage is indissoluble. Discuss.

8. In what sense is the family "a school for human enrichment"?

9. What role is the priest called upon to play in furthering the development of the family?

10. The Constitution mentions "various organizations" and "family associations" that prepare young married people to live a family, social and apostolic life. Discuss some of those with which you are familiar.

CHAPTER II

THE PROPER DEVELOPMENT OF CULTURE

Introduction

53. One of the characteristics of the human person is that he can only achieve authentic and full humanity by means of culture—that is, through the cultivation of the goods and values of nature. Therefore, whenever human life is involved, nature and culture are intimately linked together.

The word "culture" in the general sense refers to all those factors by which man refines and develops his manifold spiritual and physical qualities. He strives to subdue the earth by his knowledge and his labor; he humanizes social life on the levels of the family and the whole civic community through the improvement of customs and institutions; he expresses through his works the great spiritual experiences and aspirations of men throughout the ages, and he communicates and preserves them to be an inspiration for the progress of many, even of all mankind.

Hence it follows that culture necessarily has historical and social overtones, and the word "culture" often carries with it sociological and ethnological connotations; in this sense one can speak about the plurality of cultures. For different styles of living and different scales of values originate in different ways of using things, of working and self-expression, of practicing religion and behavior, of establishing laws and juridical institutions, of developing science and the arts and of cultivating beauty. Thus the heritage of its institutions forms the patrimony proper to each human community; a well-defined historical milieu is created which envelops every man, no matter what his epoch or nation, and from which he draws the values needed to foster humanity and civilization.

I

THE CULTURAL SITUATION TODAY

New Forms of Living

54. The circumstances of life today have undergone such profound changes on the social and cultural level that one is entitled to speak of a new age of human history; [123] hence new overtones are opened up for the development and diffusion of culture. The factors which have occasioned it have been the tremendous expansion of the natural and human sciences (including social sciences), the increase of technology and the advances in developing and organizing media of communication. As a result modern culture is characterized as follows: the "exact" sciences produce a highly critical judgment; recent psychological advances furnish deeper insights into human behavior; historical studies tend to make us view things under the aspects of changeability and evolution; customs and patterns of life tend to become more uniform from day to day; industrialization, urbanization and other factors influencing com-

---

[123] Cf. the introductory statement of this Constitution, nn. 4ff.

munity living create new mass cultures which give birth to new patterns of thinking, acting and the use of leisure; heightened media of exchange between nations and different branches of society open up the riches of different cultures to each and every individual, with the result that a more universal form of culture is gradually taking shape and through it the unity of mankind is being fostered and expressed to the degree that the particular characteristics of each culture is preserved.

Man, Author of Culture

55. In each nation and social group there is a growing number of men and women who are conscious that they themselves are the craftsmen and molders of their community's culture. All over the world the sense of autonomy and responsibility increases with effects of the greatest importance for the spiritual and moral maturity of mankind. This will become clearer to us if we place before our eyes the unification of the world and the duty imposed on us to build up a better world in truth and justice. Thus we are witnessing the birth of a new humanism where man is defined before all else by his responsibility to his brothers and to history.

Difficulties and Duties

56. In circumstances such as these it is no wonder that man feels responsible for the progress of culture and nourishes high hopes for it, but he anxiously foresees numerous conflicting elements which it is up to him to resolve.

What is to be done to prevent increased exchanges between cultures (which ought to lead to genuine and fruitful dialogue between groups and nations) from disturbing the life of communities, overthrowing traditional wisdom and endangering the character proper to each people?

How are the dynamism and expansion of the new culture to be fostered without losing living fidelity to the heritage of tradition? This question is of particular relevance in a culture where the enormous progress of science and technique must be harmonized with a system where classical studies according to various traditions have held sway.

How is the rapid and increasing specialization in different subjects to be reconciled with their very necessary synthesis, not to mention the need to safeguard man's powers of contemplation and wonder which lead to wisdom?

What can be done to enable everyone to share in the benefits of culture when the culture of specialists is becoming every day more complex and esoteric?

Finally, how are we to acknowledge as lawful the claims of autonomy which culture makes for itself without falling into a humanism which is purely earthbound and even hostile to religion?

In spite of these conflicting issues, human culture must evolve today in such a way that it will develop the whole human person harmoniously and integrally and help all men to fulfill the tasks to which they are called, especially Christians who are fraternally united at the heart of the human family.

II

SOME PRINCIPLES FOR
PROPER CULTURAL DEVELOPMENT

Faith and Culture

57. In their pilgrimage to the heavenly city

Christians are to seek and relish the things that are above.[124] This involves not a lesser but rather a greater commitment to working with all men toward the establishment of a world that is more human. Indeed, the mystery of the Christian faith provides them with an outstanding incentive and encouragement to fulfill their role even more eagerly and to discover the full sense of the commitment by which human culture becomes important in man's total vocation.

By the work of his hands and with the aid of technical means man develops the earth so that it can bear fruit and become a dwelling place worthy of mankind; he also consciously plays his part in the life of social groups. In so doing he is realizing the design, revealed by God at the beginning of time, to subdue the earth [125] and perfect the work of creation, and at the same time he is improving his own person; he is also observing the command of Christ to develop himself to the service of his fellowmen.

Furthermore, when man works in the fields of philosophy, history, mathematics and science and cultivates the arts, he can greatly contribute toward bringing the human race to a higher understanding of truth, goodness and beauty and to points of view having universal value; thus man will be more clearly enlightened by the wondrous wisdom which was with God from eternity, working beside him like a master craftsman, rejoicing in his inhabited world and delighting in the sons of men.[126] As a consequence the human spirit, freed from the bondage of material things, can be more easily drawn to the worship and contemplation of

---

124 Cf. Col. 3, 1-2.
125 Cf. Gen. 1, 28.
126 Cf. Prov. 8, 30-31.

the creator. Moreover, man is disposed to acknowledge, under the impulse of grace, the Word of God, who was in the world as "the true light that enlightens every man" (Jn. 1, 9) before becoming flesh to save and gather up all things in himself.[127]

There is no doubt that modern scientific and technical progress can lead to a certain phenomenalism or agnosticism; this happens when scientific methods of investigation, which of themselves are incapable of penetrating to the deepest nature of things, are unjustifiably taken as the supreme norm for arriving at truth. There is a further danger that in his excessive confidence in modern inventions man may think he is sufficient unto himself and give up the search for higher values.

But these drawbacks are not necessarily due to modern culture and they should not tempt us to overlook its positive values. Among these values we would like to draw attention to the following: study of the sciences and exact fidelity to truth in scientific investigation, the necessity of teamwork in technology, the sense of international solidarity, a growing awareness of the expert's responsibility to help and defend his fellowmen and an eagerness to improve the standard of living of all men, especially of those who are deprived of responsibility or suffer from cultural destitution. All these can afford a certain kind of preparation for the acceptance of the message of the Gospel and can be infused with divine charity by him who came to save the world.

---

[127] Cf. St. Irenaeus, *Adversus haereses* III, 11, 8, p. 200 (ed. Sagnard); cf. *ibid.*, 16, 6, pp. 290-92; 21, 10-22, pp. 370-72; 22, 3, p. 378; etc.

Manifold Relation between Culture and the Good News of Christ

58. There are many links between the message of salvation and culture. In his self-revelation to his people culminating in the fullness of manifestation in his incarnate Son, God spoke according to the culture proper to each age. Similarly, the Church has existed through the centuries in varying circumstances and has utilized the resources of different cultures in her preaching to spread and explain the message of Christ, to examine and understand it more deeply, and to express it more perfectly in the liturgy and in various aspects of the life of the faithful.

Nevertheless, the Church has been sent to all ages and nations; therefore, she is not tied exclusively and indissolubly to any race or nation, to any one particular way of life, or to any customary practices, ancient or modern. The Church is faithful to her traditions and is at the same time conscious of her universal mission; thus she can enter into communion with different forms of culture, thereby enriching both herself and those cultures.

The Good News of Christ continually renews the life and culture of fallen man; it combats and removes the error and evil which flows from the ever-present attraction of sin. It never ceases to purify and elevate the morality of peoples. It takes the spiritual qualities and endowments of every age and nation and with supernatural riches it causes them to blossom, as it were, from within; it thus fortifies, completes and restores them in Christ.[128] In this way the Church carries out her mission [129] and in that very act she stimulates and

---

[128] Cf. Eph. 1, 10.
[129] Cf. the words of Pius XI to Fr. M.-D. Roland-Gosselin:

advances human and civil culture, thus contributing by her activity, including liturgical activity, to man's interior freedom.

Proper Harmony between Forms of Culture

59.   For the reasons given above the Church recalls to mind that culture must be subordinated to the integral development of the human person, the good of the community and all mankind. Therefore, one must aim at encouraging the human spirit to develop its faculties of wonder, understanding, contemplation, forming personal judgments and cultivating a religious, moral and social sense.

Culture, since it flows from man's rational and social nature, has continual need of rightful freedom of development and a legitimate possibility of autonomy according to its own principles. Quite rightly it demands respect and enjoys a certain inviolability, provided, of course, that the rights of the individual and the community, both particular and universal, are safeguarded within the limits of the common good.

Calling to mind the teaching of Vatican Council I, this sacred Synod declares that "there are two orders of knowledge" distinct from one another—namely, faith and reason—and that the Church is not opposed to "the use by human arts and sciences of their own principles and methods in their respective fields"; therefore, "she acknowledges this lawful freedom" and affirms the legitimate autonomy of culture and especially of the sciences.[130]

"It is necessary never to lose sight of the fact that the objective of the Church is to evangelize, not to civilize. If she civilizes, it is for the sake of evangelization": *Semaines sociales de France* (Versailles, 1936), pp. 461-62.

[130] Cf. Vatican Council I, *Dogmatic Constitution on the Catholic Faith*: *Denz.* 1795, 1799 (3015, 3019). Cf. also Pius

All this demands that man, provided he respects the moral order and the common good, is entitled to seek after truth, express and make known his opinions; he may practice whatever art he pleases; finally, he ought to be truthfully informed about matters of public interest.[131]

The scope of public authority does not extend to determining the proper nature or forms of human culture, but rather to building up the environment and the provision of assistance favorable to the development of culture, without overlooking minority groups in the nation.[132] This is the reason why one must avoid at all costs distorting culture from its proper purpose and its exploitation by political or economic powers.

III

SOME MORE URGENT DUTIES OF CHRISTIANS IN REGARD TO CULTURE

Recognition of Everyone's Right to Culture and Its Implementation

60. Man is now offered the possibility to free most of the human race from the curse of ignorance; therefore, it is one of the duties most appropriate to our times, particularly for Christians, to work untiringly for fundamental decisions to be taken in economic and political affairs, on the national as well as the international level, which will ensure the recognition and implementation everywhere of the right of every man to human and civil

---

XI, Encyclical Letter *Quadragesimo anno*: *A.A.S.* 23 (1931), p. 190.

131 Cf. John XXIII, Encyclical Letter *Pacem in terris*: *A.A.S.* 55 (1963), p. 260.

132 Cf. *ibid.*, p. 283; cf. also Pius XII, Radio Address of Dec. 24, 1941: *A.A.S.* 34 (1942), pp. 16-7.

culture in harmony with the dignity of the human person, without distinction of race, sex, nation, religion or social circumstances. Hence it is necessary to ensure that there is a sufficiency of cultural benefits available to everyone, especially the benefit of what is called "basic" culture, lest any man be prevented by illiteracy and lack of initiative from contributing in an authentically human way to the common good.

Every effort should be made to provide those who are capable with the opportunity to pursue higher studies; such planning should be so organized that as far as possible those students will engage in the functions and services and play the role in society most in keeping with their talents and the skills they acquire.[133] In this way every individual and social groups of every people will be able to attain a full development of their cultural life in harmony with their capabilities and their traditions.

We must do everything possible to make everyone aware of their right to culture and their duty to develop themselves culturally and to help their fellows. Sometimes conditions of life and work are such as to stifle man's cultural efforts and destroy his taste for culture. This holds true especially for those living in the country and for manual workers who ought to be provided with working conditions not unfavorable, but rather conducive to, their cultural development. At present women are involved in nearly all spheres of life; they ought to be permitted to play their part fully according to their own particular nature. Everyone should acknowledge and foster the proper and necessary participation of women in cultural life.

---

[133] Cf. John XXIII, Encyclical Letter *Pacem in terris: A.A.S.* 55 (1963), p. 260.

Cultural Training

61. Nowadays, much more than in the past, it is difficult to form a synthesis of the arts and of the different branches of knowledge. While, in fact, the volume and diversity of the constituent elements of culture are on the increase, there is a decrease in the individual's capability to perceive and harmonize them; as a result the picture of "a universal man" has almost disappeared. Nevertheless, it remains each man's duty to safeguard the notion of the human person as a totality in which values of intellect, will, conscience, and brotherhood predominate, since these values were established by the creator and wondrously restored and elevated by Christ.

Training of this kind has its source and its cradle, as it were, in the family; there, in an atmosphere of love, children learn more quickly the true scale of values, and approved forms of culture are almost naturally assimilated by the developing minds of adolescents.

There are nowadays many opportunities favorable to the development of a universal culture, thanks especially to the boom in book publication and new techniques of cultural and social communication. Shorter working hours are becoming the general rule everywhere and provide greater opportunities for large numbers of people. May this leisure time be properly employed to refresh the spirit and strengthen the health of mind and body —by means of voluntary activity and study, by tourism to broaden the mind and enrich man with understanding of others, and by physical exercise and sport which help to create harmony of feeling even on the level of the community as well as foster friendly relations between men of all classes, countries and races. Christians, therefore, should cooperate in the cultural framework and collective activity characteristic of our times to humanize them and imbue them with a Christian spirit. All these advantages, however, are insufficient to confer full cultural development unless they are accompanied by a deeply thought-out evaluation of the meaning of culture and knowledge for the human person.

Proper Harmony between Culture and Christian Thought

62. Although the Church has contributed largely to the progress of culture, it is the lesson of experience that arising out of contingent factors there have been difficulties in the way of harmonizing culture with Christian thought. These difficulties do not necessarily harm the life of faith. Indeed, they can stimulate the mind to a deeper and more precise understanding of that faith. In fact, recent research and discoveries in the sciences, history and philosophy bring up new problems which have an important bearing on life itself and demand new scrutiny by theologians. Furthermore, theologians are now being asked, within the methods and limits of the science of theology, to seek more efficient ways of presenting their teaching to modern man. The deposit and the truths of faith are one thing; the manner of expressing them is quite another, provided the meaning and understanding of them is safeguarded.[134] In pastoral care sufficient use should be made not only of theological principles but also of the findings of secular sciences, especially psychology and sociology; in this way the faithful will be brought to a purer and more mature living of the faith.

[134] Cf. John XXIII, prayer delivered on Oct. 11, 1962, at the opening of Vatican Council II: *A.A.S.* 54 (1964), p. 792.

In their own way literature and art are very important in the life of the Church. They seek to give expression to man's nature, his problems and his experience in an effort to discover and perfect man himself and the world in which he lives; they try to discover his place in history and in the universe, to throw light on his suffering and his joy, his needs and his potentialities, and to outline a happier destiny in store for him. Hence they can elevate human life, which they express under many forms according to various times and places.

Every effort should therefore be made to make artists feel that they are understood by the Church in their artistic work and to encourage them, while enjoying a reasonable standard of freedom, to enter into happier relations with the Christian community. New art forms adapted to our times and in keeping with the characteristics of different nations and regions should be acknowledged by the Church. They may also be brought into the sanctuary whenever they raise the mind up to God with suitable forms of expression and are in conformity with liturgical requirements.[135] Thus the knowledge of God will be made better known, and the preaching of the Gospel will be rendered more intelligible to man's mind and appear more relevant to his situation.

Therefore, the faithful ought to work in close conjunction with their contemporaries and try to get to know their ways of thinking and feeling as they find them expressed in current culture. Let the faithful incorporate the findings of new sciences and teachings and the understanding of the most recent discoveries with Christian morality

---

135 Cf. Vatican Council II, *Constitution on the Sacred Liturgy*, n. 123: *A.A.S.* 56 (1964), p. 131; Paul VI, *Discourse to the Artists of Rome: A.A.S.* 56 (1964), pp. 439-42.

and thought so that their practice of religion and their moral behavior may keep abreast of their acquaintance with science and of the relentless progress of technology; in this way they will succeed in evaluating and interpreting everything with an authentically Christian sense of values.

Those involved in theological studies in seminaries and universities should be eager to cooperate with men versed in other fields of learning by pooling their resources and their points of view. Theological research, while it deepens knowledge of revealed truth, should not lose contact with its own times, so that experts in various fields may be led to a deeper knowledge of the faith. Collaboration of this kind will be beneficial in the formation of sacred ministers; they will be able to present teaching on God, man and the world in a way more suited to our contemporaries, who will then be more ready to accept their words.[136] Furthermore, it is to be hoped that more of the laity will receive adequate theological formation and that some among them will dedicate themselves professionally to these studies and contribute to their advancement. But for the proper exercise of this role, the faithful, both clerical and lay, should be accorded a lawful freedom of inquiry, of thought and of expression, tempered by humility and courage, in whatever branch of study they have specialized.[137]

---

[136] Cf. Vatican Council II, *Decree on Priestly Training* and *Declaration on Christian Education.*

[137] Cf. Vatican Council II, *Dogmatic Constitution on the Church*, n. 37: *A.A.S.* 57 (1965), pp. 42-43.

Study-Club Questions

1. The Constitution speaks of the circumstances of present-day life as having undergone "profound changes on the social and cultural level". What are these "changes"?

2. Contemporary man is exposed to many and varied forms of pressures non-existent a half century ago. Discuss.

3. Man is the author of culture. Explain. Discuss the relation between faith and culture.

4. Does modern scientific and technical progress necessarily lead to atheism?

5. How does the Good News of Christ renew the life and culture of fallen man? Mention some ways in which the Church has contributed to the development of culture in the past.

6. "The Church needs to speak to modern man in terms he can understand." Discuss.

7. In what way or ways are personal freedom and autonomy related to the development of culture?

8. It is often asserted that the Church is opposed to truly scientific inquiry. Discuss.

9. Is it possible to be a Christian and a humanist at the same time?

10. Theology is challenged as never before to present the
    Christian message more efficiently and clearly to
    modern man. What are some of the steps that
    theology can take to meet this challenge successfully?

CHAPTER III

Economic and Social Life

Some Characteristics of Economic Life Today

63.   In the sphere of economics and social life too, the dignity and entire vocation of the human person and the welfare of society as a whole have to be respected and fostered, for man is the source, the focus and the end of all economic and social life.

Like all other areas of social life, the economy of today is marked by man's growing dominion over nature, by closer and keener relationships between individuals, groups and peoples, and by the frequency of State intervention. At the same time increased efficiency in production and improved methods of distribution, productivity and services have rendered the economy an instrument capable of meeting the growing needs of the human family.

But the picture is not without its disturbing elements. Many people, especially in economically advanced areas, seem to be dominated by economics; almost all of their personal and social lives are permeated with a kind of economic mentality, and this is true of nations that favor a collective economy as well as of other nations. At the very time when economic progress (provided it is directed and organized in a reasonable and human way)

183

could do so much to reduce social inequalities, it serves all too often only to aggravate them; in some places it even leads to a decline in the position of the underprivileged and contempt for the poor. In the midst of vast numbers of people deprived of the absolute necessities of life there are some who live in luxury and squander their wealth, and this happens in less developed areas as well. Luxury and misery exist side by side. While a few individuals enjoy an almost unlimited opportunity to choose for themselves, the vast majority have no chance whatever of exercising personal initiative and responsibility, and quite often they have to live and work in conditions unworthy of human beings.

Similar economic and social imbalances exist between those engaged in agriculture, industry and the service industries, and even between different areas of the same country. The growing contrast between the economically more advanced countries and others could well endanger world peace.

Our contemporaries are daily becoming more keenly aware of these discrepancies because they are thoroughly convinced that this unhappy state of affairs can and should be rectified by the greater technical and economic resources available in the words, of all elements which contirbute to economic and social life is required, together with a change of mentality and attitude by all men. It was for this reason that the Church in the course of the centuries has worked out in the light of the Gospel principles of justice and equity demanded by right reason for individual and social life and also for international relations. The Council now intends to reiterate these principles in accordance with the situation of the world today and will outline certain guidelines, particularly with reference to the requirements of economic development.[138]

I

ECONOMIC DEVELOPMENT

Economic Development in the Service of Man

64. Today more than ever before there is an increase in the production of agricultural and industrial goods and in the number of services available. This is as it should be in view of population expansion and growing human aspirations. Therefore, we must encourage technical progress and the spirit of enterprise, we must foster the eagerness for creativity and improvement, and we must promote adaptation of production methods and all serious efforts of people engaged in production—in other words, of all elements which contribute to economic progress. The ultimate and basic objective of economic production does not consist merely in the increase of goods produced or in profit or prestige; it is directed rather to the service of man—the whole man, taking into account his material needs and the requirements of his intellectual, moral, spiritual and religious life. This applies to every man and to every group of men in every part of the world, no matter what their status or race. Therefore, economic activity is to be carried out in accordance with techniques and methods belong-

---

138 Cf. Pius XII, Address of March 23, 1952: *A.A.S.* 44 (1952), p. 273; John XXIII, *Allocution to the Catholic Association of Italian Workers*, May 1, 1959: *A.A.S.* 51 (1959), p. 358.

ing to the moral order [139] so that God's design for man may be fulfilled.[140]

Economic Development under Man's Direction

65.   Economic development must remain under man's direction; it is not to be left to the judgment of a few individuals or groups possessing too much economic power, nor of the political community alone, nor of a few strong nations. It is necessary that, in matters of general interest, as many people as possible—and, where international relations are concerned, all nations—should participate actively in the direction of that development. Moreover, the voluntary efforts of individuals and of free groups should be properly coordinated and harmoniously joined with the undertakings of public authorities. Nor should development be left to the almost mechanical evolution of economic activity or to the decision of public authority. Hence we must denounce as false those doctrines which stand in the way of all reform on the pretext of a false notion of freedom, as well as those which subordinate the fundamental rights of individuals and of groups to the collective organization of production.[141]

---

[139] Cf. Pius XI, Encyclical Letter *Quadragesimo anno*: *A.A.S.* 23 (1931), pp. 190ff.; Pius XII, Address of March 23, 1952: *A.A.S.* 44 (1952), pp. 276ff.; John XXIII, Encyclical Letter *Mater et Magistra*: *A.A.S.* 53 (1961), p. 450; Vatican Council II, *Decree on the Instruments of Social Communication*, n. 6: *A.A.S.* 56 (1964), p. 147.

[140] Cf. Mt. 16, 26; Lk. 16, 1-31; Col. 3, 17.

[141] Cf. Leo XIII, Encyclical Letter *Libertas*: *Acta Leonis XIII*, t. VIII, pp. 220ff.; Pius XI, Encyclical Letter *Quadragesimo anno*: *A.A.S.* 23 (1931), pp. 191ff.; Pius XI, Encyclical Letter *Divini redemptoris*: *A.A.S.* 29 (1937), pp. 65ff.; Pius XII, Christmas Message of 1941: *A.A.S.* 34 (1942), pp. 10ff.; John XXIII, Encyclical Letter *Mater et Magistra*: *A.A.S.* 53 (1961), pp. 401-64.

All citizens should remember that they have the right and the duty to contribute according to their ability to the genuine progress of their own community, and this must be recognized by the civil authority. Particularly in areas of retarded economic progress, where all resources must be urgently exploited, the common good is seriously endangered by those who hoard their resources unproductively and by those who (apart from the case of every man's personal right of migration) deprive their community of much needed material and spiritual assistance.

An End to Excessive Economic and Social Differences

66. To fulfill the requirements of justice and equity, every effort must be made to put an end as soon as possible to the immense economic inequalities which exist in the world and increase from day to day, as well as to individual and social discrimination, provided, of course, that the rights of individuals and the character of each people are not disturbed. Likewise in many areas, in view of the special difficulties of production and marketing in agriculture, country people must be helped to improve methods of production and marketing, to introduce necessary developments and renewal, and to achieve a fair return of their products, lest they continue, as often happens, in the state of secondary citizens. Farmers themselves, especially young farmers, ought to apply themselves eagerly to bettering their professional skill, without which the advancement of farming is impossible.[142]

Justice and equity also demand that the livelihood of individuals and their families should not

---

[142] In reference to agricultural problems, cf. especially John XXIII, Encyclical Letter *Mater et Magistra*: *A.A.S.* 53 (1961), pp. 341ff.

become insecure and precarious through a kind of mobility which is a necessary feature of developing economies. All kinds of discrimination in wages and working conditions should be avoided in regard to workers who come from other countries or areas and contribute by their work to the economic development of a people or a region. Furthermore, no one, especially public authorities, should treat them simply as mere tools of production rather than as persons; they should facilitate matters so that they may have their families with them and be able to acquire decent housing conditions, and they should endeavor to integrate them into the social life of the country or area to which they have come. However, employment should be found for them in their own countries whenever possible.

Nowadays when the economy is undergoing transition—as in new forms of industrialization where, for example, automation is being introduced—care must be taken to ensure that there is sufficient and suitable employment available; opportunities for appropriate technical and professional training should be provided and safeguards should be established to protect the livelihood and human dignity of those who labor under serious disadvantages because of age or ill-health.

II

SOME PRINCIPLES GOVERNING SOCIO-ECONOMIC LIFE AS A WHOLE

Work, Working Conditions, Leisure

67. Human labor which is expended in the production and exchange of goods or in the provision of economic services is superior to all other

elements of economic life, for the latter are only means to an end.

Whether exercised independently or in subordination to another, human labor proceeds from the human person who, as it were, impresses his seal on the things of nature and reduces them to his will. By his work a man ordinarily provides for himself and his family, associates with others as his brothers and renders them service; in this way he can exercise genuine charity and be a partner in the work of bringing divine creation to perfection. Moreover, we believe by faith that, through the homage of work offered to God, man is associated with the redemptive work of Jesus Christ whose labor with his hands at Nazareth greatly ennobled the dignity of work. This is the source of every man's duty to work faithfully, as well as the basis of his right to work; moreover, it is the duty of society, according to the prevailing circumstances, to see to it that all citizens have the opportunity of finding employment. Finally, remuneration for work should guarantee man the opportunity to provide a dignified livelihood for himself and his family on the material, social, cultural and spiritual level to correspond to the role and the productivity of each, the relevant economic factors in his employment, and the common good.[143]

Since economic activity is, for the most part, the

---

143 Cf. Leo XIII, Encyclical Letter *Rerum novarum*: *A.A.S.* 23 (1890-91), pp. 649, 662; Pius XI, Encyclical Letter *Quadragesimo anno*: *A.A.S.* 23 (1931), pp. 200-1; Pius XI, Encyclical Letter *Divini redemptoris*: *A.A.S.* 29 (1937), p. 92; Pius XII, Radio Address on Christmas Eve, 1942: *A.A.S.* 35 (1943), p. 20; Pius XII, Allocution of June 13, 1943: *A.A.S.* 35 (1943), p. 172; Pius XII, Radio Address to the Workers of Spain, March 11, 1951: *A.A.S.* 43 (1951), p. 215; John XXIII, Encyclical Letter *Mater et Magistra*: *A.A.S.* 53 (1961), p. 419.

fruit of the collaboration of many men, it is unjust and inhuman to organize and direct it in such a way that some workers are exploited. But it frequently happens, even today, that workers are almost enslaved by the work they do. Under no circumstances can this fact be justified by so-called laws of economics. Therefore, the entire process of productive work must be adapted to the needs of the human person and to his way of life, with special attention to domestic life and mothers of families in particular, always taking sex and age into account. Workers should have the opportunity to develop their talents and their personality through the performance of their work. While devoting their time and energy to the performance of their work with a due sense of responsibility, they should also be allowed sufficient rest and leisure to cultivate their family, cultural, social and religious life. In addition, they should be given the opportunity to develop those energies and talents to which their professional work may perhaps give little scope.

Responsibility-Sharing in Enterprise and in the Economic System as a Whole; Labor Disputes

68. In business enterprises it is persons who associate together—that is, free and autonomous men who are created in the image of God. Therefore, while taking into account the role of every person concerned—owners, employers, management and employees—and without weakening the necessary executive unity, the active participation of everyone in the responsibility of administration is to be encouraged.[144] More often, however, de-

---

[144] Cf. John XXIII, Encyclical Letter *Mater et Magistra*: *A.A.S.* 53 (1961), pp. 408, 424, 427; however, the word "curatione" has been taken from the Latin text of the Encyclical Letter *Quadragesimo anno*: *A.A.S.* 23 (1931), p.

cisions concerning economic and social conditions are made not so much within the business itself as by institutions at a higher level, and since it is on these that the future of the workers and their children depends, the workers themselves should also have a share in decision-making either in person or through their representatives.

Among the fundamental rights of the individual must be numbered the right of workers to form themselves into associations which truly represent them and are able to cooperate in organizing economic life properly. Included is the right to freely take part in the activities of such associations without fear of reprisal. Through such organized participation, together with progressive economic and social formation, there will be a growing awareness among all people of their role and their responsibility, and, according to their capacities and aptitudes, they will come to realize that they have an active part to play in the whole task of economic and social development and in the achievement of the universal common good.

In the event of economic-social disputes all should strive to achieve peaceful settlements. The first step is to engage in sincere discussion between all sides, but the right to strike remains even in the circumstances of today a necessary (although an ultimate) means for the defense of workers' rights and the satisfaction of their lawful aspirations. As soon as possible, however, avenues should be explored to resume negotiations and effect reconciliation.

---

199. In regard to the evolution of the question, cf. also Pius XII, Allocution of June 3, 1950: *A.A.S.* 42 (1950), pp. 485-88; Paul VI, Allocution of June 8, 1964: *A.A.S.* 56 (1964), pp. 574-79.

Earthly Goods Destined for All Men

69.   God destined the earth and everything it contains for the use of all men and all peoples so that all created things would be shared fairly by all mankind under the guidance of justice tempered by charity.[145] No matter what the structures of property are in different nations, according to various and changing circumstances and adapted to their lawful institutions, we must never lose sight of this universal destination of earthly goods. In his use of things man should regard the external goods he legitimately owns not merely as exclusive to himself but common to others also, in the sense that they can benefit others as well as himself.[146] Therefore, every man has the right to possess a sufficient amount of the earth's goods for himself and his family. This has been the opinion of the Fathers and Doctors of the Church who taught that men are bound to come to the aid of the poor and to do so not merely out of their superfluous goods.[147] When a person is in extreme

---

[145] Cf. Pius XII, Encyclical Letter *Sertum laetitiae*: *A.A.S.* 31 (1939), p. 642; John XXIII, Consistorial Allocution: *A.A.S.* 52 (1960), pp. 5-11; John XXIII, Encyclical Letter *Mater et Magistra*: *A.A.S.* 53 (1961), p. 411.

[146] Cf. St. Thomas, *Summa Theologica* II-II, q. 32, a. 5 ad 2; *ibid.*, p. 66, a. 2; cf. explanation in Encyclical Letter of Leo XIII, *Rerum novarum*: *A.A.S.* 23 (1890-91), p. 651; cf. also Pius XII, Allocution of June 1, 1941: *A.A.S.* 33 (1941), p. 199; Pius XII, Christmas Radio Address of 1954: *A.A.S.* 47 (1955), p. 27.

[147] Cf. St. Basil, *Hom. in illud Lucae "Destruam horrea mea"*, n. 2: *P.G.* 31, 263; Lactantius, *Divinarum Institutionum*, V, on justice: *P.L.* 6, 565B; St. Augustine, *In Ioann. Ev.*, tr. 50, n. 6: *P.L.* 35, 1760; St. Augustine, *Enarratio in Ps. CXLVII*, 12: *P.L.* 37, 192; St. Gregory the Great, *Homiliae in Ev.*, hom. 20: *P.L.* 76, 1165; St. Gregory the Great, *Regulae Pastoralis liber*, part III, c. 21: *P.L.* 77, 87; St. Bonaventure, *In III Sent.*, d. 33, dub. 1: (ed. Quarac-

necessity he has the right to supply himself with what he needs out of the riches of others.[148] Faced with a world today where so many people are suffering from want, the Council asks individuals and peoples to remember the saying of the Fathers: "Feed the man dying of hunger, because if you do not feed him you are killing him"; [149] it further urges each one according to his ability to share and dispose of his goods to help others, above all by giving them aid which will enable them to help and develop themselves.

In economically less developed societies it often happens that the common destination of goods is partly achieved by a system of community customs and traditions which guarantee a minimum of necessities to each one. Certain customs must not

chi III, 728) ; St. Bonaventure, *In IV Sent.*, d. 15, p. II, a. 2, q. 1: (ed. *cit.*, IV, 371b) ; q. *de superfluo* (ms. *Assisi Bibl. comun.* 186, ff. 112ª-113ª) ; St. Albert the Great, *In III Sent.*, d. 33, a. 3, sol. 1: (ed. Borgnet XXVIII, 611) ; St. Albert the Great, *In IV Sent.*, d. 15, a. 16 (ed. *cit.*, XXIX, 494-97). As for the determination of what is superfluous in our day and age, cf. John XXIII, Radio and Television Message of Sept. 11, 1962: *A.A.S.* 54 (1962) , p. 682: "The obligation of every man, the urgent obligation of the Christian man, is to reckon what is superfluous by the measure of the needs of others and to see to it that the administration and the distribution of created goods serve the common good."

148 In this case, the old principle holds true: "In extreme necessity all goods are common: that is, all goods are to be shared." On the other hand, for the order, extension and manner in which the principle is applied in the proposed text, besides the modern authors cf. St. Thomas, *Summa Theologica* II-II, q. 66, a. 7. Obviously, for the correct application of the principle, all the conditions that are morally required must be met.

149 Cf. Gratian, *Decretum*, c. 21, dist. LXXXVI: ed. Friedberg I, 302. This axiom is previously found in *P.L.* 54, 591A (cf. *Antonianum* 27 [1952], pp. 349-66).

be considered sacrosanct if they no longer correspond to modern needs; on the other hand one should not rashly do away with respectable customs which, if they are brought up to date, can still be very useful. In the same way in economically advanced countries the common destination of goods is achieved through a system of social institutions dealing with insurance and security. Family and social services, especially those providing for culture and education, should be further developed. In setting up these different organizations, care must be taken to prevent the citizens from slipping into a kind of passivity vis-à-vis society, or of irresponsibility in their duty, or of a refusal to do their fair share.

Investment and Money

70. Investment in its turn should be directed to providing employment and ensuring sufficient income for the active population both in the present and for the future. Whoever is responsible for investments and the planning of the economy (individuals, associations and public authority) must keep these objectives in mind; they must show themselves aware of their serious obligation, on the one hand, to see to it that the necessities for living a decent life are available to individuals and to the community as a whole, and, on the other hand, to provide for the future and strike a rightful balance between the needs of present-day consumption, both individual and collective, and the requirements of investment for future generations. Always before their eyes they must keep the pressing needs of underdeveloped countries and areas. In fiscal matters they must be careful not to do harm to their own country or to any other country. Care must also be taken that economically weak coun-

tries do not suffer unduly from the devaluation of currency.

Ownership, Private Property, Large Estates

71. Since property and other forms of private ownership of external goods contribute to the expression of personality and provide man with the opportunity to exercise his role in society and in the economy, it is very important that the access of both individuals and communities to some form of ownership of external goods be fostered.

Private property or some form of ownership of external goods assures a person a highly necessary sphere for the exercise of his personal and family autonomy and should be considered as an extension of human freedom. Lastly, in stimulating the exercise of responsibility, it constitutes one of the prerequisites of civil liberties. [150] Nowadays the forms of such ownership or property are varied and are becoming more diversified every day. In spite of the social security, the rights and the services guaranteed by society, all these forms of ownership are still a source of security which must not be underestimated. This applies not only to ownership of material goods but also to the possession of professional skills.

The lawfulness of private ownership is not opposed to the various forms of public ownership. But the transfer of goods from private to public

---

[150] Cf. Leo XIII, Encyclical Letter *Rerum novarum*: *A.A.S.* 23 (1890-91), pp. 643-46; Pius XI Encyclical Letter *Quadragesimo anno*: *A.A.S.* 23 (1931), p. 191; Pius XII, Radio Message of June 1, 1941: *A.A.S.* 33 (1941), p. 199; Pius XII, Radio Message of Christmas Eve, 1942: *A.A.S.* 35 (1943), p. 17; Pius XII, Radio Message of Sept. 1, 1944: *A.A.S.* 36 (1944), p. 253; John XXIII, Encyclical Letter *Mater et Magistra*: *A.A.S.* 53 (1961), pp. 428-29.

ownership may only be undertaken by competent authority, in accordance with the demands and within the limits of the common good, and it must be accompanied by adequate compensation. Furthermore, the State has the duty to prevent anyone from abusing his private property to the detriment of the common good.[151] By its nature private property has a social dimension which is based on the law of the common destination of earthly goods.[152] Whenever the social aspect is forgotten, ownership can often become the source of greed and serious disorder so that its opponents easily find a pretext for calling the right itself into question.

In several economically retarded areas there exist large and sometimes very extensive rural estates which are only slightly cultivated or not cultivated at all for the sake of profit, while the majority of the population have no land or possess only very small holdings and the need to increase agricultural production is pressing and evident to all. Not infrequently those who are hired as laborers or who till a portion of the land as tenants receive a wage or income unworthy of a human being; moreover, they are often deprived of decent living conditions and are exploited by middlemen. They lack all sense of security and live in such a state of personal dependence that almost all chance of exercising initiative and responsibility is closed to them and any cultural advancement and participation in social and political life is non-existent. Reforms are called for in these different situations: incomes must be raised, working conditions im-

---

151 Cf. Pius XI, Encyclical Letter *Quadragesimo anno: A.A.S.* 23 (1931), p. 214; John XXIII, Encyclical Letter *Mater et Magistra: A.A.S.* 53 (1961), p. 429.
152 Cf. Pius XII, Radio Message of Pentecost, 1941: *A.A.S.* 44 (1941), p. 199; John XXIII, Encyclical Letter *Mater et Magistra: A.A.S.* 53 (1961), p. 430.

proved, security in employment assured and personal incentives to work encouraged; estates insufficiently cultivated must even be divided up and given to those who will be able to make them productive. In this event the necessary resources and equipment must be supplied, especially educational facilities and proper cooperative organizations. However, when the common good calls for expropriation, compensation must be made and is to be calculated according to equity, with all circumstances taken into account.

Economic and Social Activity and the Kingdom of Christ

72. Christians actively engaged in modern economic and social progress and in the struggle for justice and charity must be convinced that they have much to contribute to the prosperity of mankind and to world peace. Let them, as individuals and as group members, give a shining example to others. Endowed with the skill and experience so absolutely necessary for them, let them preserve a proper sense of values in their earthly activity in loyalty to Christ and his Gospel in order that their entire lives, individual as well as social, may be inspired by the spirit of the beatitudes, and in particular by the spirit of poverty.

Anyone who in obedience to Christ seeks first the kingdom of God will derive from it a stronger and a purer love for helping all his brethren and for accomplishing the task of justice under the inspiration of charity.[153]

---

[153] For the right use of goods according to the doctrine of the New Testament, cf. Lk. 3, 11; 10, 30ff.; 11, 41; 1 Pet. 5, 3; Mk. 8, 36; 12, 39-41; Jas. 5, 1-6; 1 Tim. 6, 8; Eph. 4, 28; 2 Cor. 8, 13; 1. Jn. 3, 17ff.

Study-Club Questions

1. Why does economic imbalance among countries endanger world peace?

2. What moral techniques should govern economic activity?

3. Man is responsible for his economic development. Discuss.

4. What steps can be taken to correct the economic inequalities that exist in our own country?

5. Why is the right of workers to form themselves into associations considered a fundamental right?

6. What are some of the difficulties inherent in exercising such a right?

7. Discuss the right to strike. Is it always a right?

8. Should workers ever be legally forced to return to work?

9. "When a person is in extreme necessity he has the right to supply himself with what he needs out of the riches of others." Discuss.

10. What is the Church's role in ensuring economic equality throughout the world? How does this relate to her mission to establish the kingdom of God on earth?

CHAPTER IV

THE POLITICAL COMMUNITY

Modern Public Life

73. In our times profound transformations are to be noticed in the structures and institutions of peoples; they are the accompaniment of cultural, economic and social development. These transformations exercise a deep influence on political life, particularly in regard to the rights and duties of the individual in the exercise of civil freedom and in the attainment of the common good; moreover, they affect the relations of citizens with each other and their position vis-à-vis the State.

A keener awareness of human dignity has given rise in various parts of the world to an eagerness to establish a politico-juridical order where the rights of the human person in public life will be better protected—for example, the right of free assembly and association, the right to express one's opinions and to profess one's religion privately and publicly. The protection of personal rights is indeed a necessary condition for citizens, individually and collectively, to play an active part in public life and administration.

Linked with cultural, economic and social progress there is a growing desire among many people to assume greater responsibilities in the organization of political life. Many people are becoming increasingly eager to ensure that the rights of minority groups in their country be safeguarded, without overlooking the duties of these minorities toward the political community; there is also an increase in tolerance for men of other opinions or religions; at the same time wider cooperation is taking place to guarantee the actual exercise of personal rights to all citizens, and not only a few privileged individuals, to exercise their rights effectively as persons.

Political systems (still prevailing in some parts of the world) are being repudiated whenever they hinder civil and religious freedom, victimize their citizens through avarice and political crimes, or distort the exercise of authority from the service of the common good to the interests of political parties or of the governing classes.

There is no better way to establish political life on a truly human basis than by encouraging an inward sense of justice, goodwill and service to the common good and by consolidating the basic convictions of men as to the true nature of the political community and the aim, proper exercise and the limits of public authority.

Nature and Purpose of the Political Community

74. Individuals, families and the various groups which comprise the civil community are aware of their inability to achieve a truly human life by their own unaided efforts; they see the need for a wider community where each one will make a specific contribution to an even broader implementation of the common good.[154] For this reason

---

[154] Cf. John XXIII, Encyclical Letter *Mater et Magistra*: *A.A.S.* 53 (1961), p. 417.

they establish various forms of political communities. The political community, then, exists for the sake of common good, in which it finds its full justification and meaning and the source of its specific and basic right to exist. The common good embraces the sum total of all those conditions of social life which enable individuals, families and organizations to achieve complete and efficacious fulfillment.[155]

The persons who comprise the political community are many and diverse; thus it is quite understandable that they may have widely differing points of view. Therefore, if the political community is not to be torn apart while everyone follows his own opinion, an authority is needed to direct the energies of all toward the common good—not in a mechanical or despotic fashion, but by acting above all as a moral force based on freedom and a sense of responsibility. It is clear that the political community and public authority are founded on human nature and, therefore, that they belong to an order established by God; nevertheless, the choice of the political regime and the appointment of rulers should be left to the free decision of the citizens.[156]

It follows that political authority, either within the political community as such or through organizations representing the State, must be exercised within the limits of the moral order and directed toward a dynamically conceived common good according to the juridical order legitimately established or due to be established. Citizens, then, are bound in conscience to obey.[157] Accordingly, the responsibility, the dignity and the importance of State rulers is clear.

---

155 Cf. *ibid.*
156 Cf. Rom. 13, 1-5.
157 Cf. Rom. 13, 5.

When citizens are under the oppression of a public authority which oversteps its competence, they should still not refuse to give or to do whatever is objectively demanded of them by the common good; but it is legitimate for them to defend their own rights and those of their fellow citizens against abuses of this authority within the limits of the natural law and the law of the Gospel.

The concrete forms of structure and organization of public authority adopted in any political community may vary according to the character of various peoples and their historical development, but their aim should always be the formation of a human person who is cultured, peace-loving and well-disposed toward his fellowmen, with a view to the benefit of the whole human race.

Collaboration by All in Public Life

75.   It is fully consonant with human nature that there should be politico-juridical structures that without any discrimination provide all citizens with ever improving and effective opportunities to play an active part in the establishment of the juridical foundations of the political community, in the administration of public affairs, in determining the aims and the terms of reference of public bodies and in the election of political leaders.[158] Every citizen should be mindful of his right and his duty to promote the common good by using his vote. The Church praises and esteems those who devote themselves to public service for the good of men and take upon themselves the burdens of public office.

---

[158] Cf. Pius XII, Radio Message of Dec. 24, 1942: *A.A.S.* 35 (1943), pp. 9-24; Pius XII, Radio Message of Dec. 24, 1944: *A.A.S.* 37 (1945), pp. 11-17; John XXIII, Encyclical Letter *Pacem in terris*: *A.A.S.* 55 (1963), pp. 263, 271, 277-78.

If the citizens' cooperation and their sense of responsibility are to produce the favorable results expected of them in the normal course of public life, a system of positive law is required providing for a suitable division of the functions and organs of public authority and an effective and independent protection of citizens' rights. The rights of all individuals, families and organizations and their practical implementation must be acknowledged, protected and fostered,[159] together with the public duties binding on all citizens. Among these duties it is worth mentioning the obligation of rendering to the State whatever material and personal services are required for the common good. Governments should take care not to put obstacles in the way of family, cultural or social groups, or of organizations and intermediate institutions, nor to hinder their lawful and constructive activity; rather, they should eagerly seek to promote such orderly activity. Citizens, on the other hand, either individually or collectively, should take care not to vest excessive power in the hands of public authority or to make untimely and exaggerated demands for concessions and subsidies, thereby lessening the sense of responsibility on the part of individuals, families and social groups.

The growing complexity of modern situations makes it necessary for public authority to intervene more often in social, cultural and economic matters in order to bring about more favorable conditions which will enable individuals and groups to pursue freely and effectively the achievement of man's well-being in its totality. The understanding

---

159 Cf. Pius XII, Radio Message of June 7, 1941: *A.A.S.* 33 (1941), p. 200; John XXIII, Encyclical Letter *Pacem in terris*: *A.A.S.* 55 (1963), pp. 273-74.

of the relationship between socialization [160] and personal autonomy and progress will vary according to different areas and the development of peoples. However, if restrictions on the exercise of human rights are temporarily imposed for the common good, these restrictions should be lifted as soon as possible after the situation has changed. In any case it is inhuman for public authority to fall back on totalitarian methods or dictatorships which violate the rights of individuals or social groups.

Citizens should cultivate a generous and loyal spirit of patriotism, but without narrow-mindedness, so that they will always keep in mind the welfare of the whole human family which is formed into one by various ties that bind races, peoples and nations.

Christians must be conscious of their specific and proper role in the political community; they should be a shining example by their sense of responsibility and their dedication to the common good; they should show in practice how authority can be reconciled with freedom, personal initiative with the solidarity and the needs of the whole social framework, and the advantages of unity with fruitful diversity. They should recognize the legitimacy of differing points of view about worldly affairs and show respect for their fellow citizens who, even in groups, defend their opinions by legitimate means. Political parties, for their part, must support whatever in their opinion is conducive to the common good; they must never put their own interests before the common good.

So that all citizens will be able to play their part in the life of the political community, civil

---

[160] Cf. John XXIII, Encyclical Letter *Mater et Magistra: A.A.S.* 53 (1961) , p. 416.

and political education is vitally necessary for the population as a whole, particularly for young people, and must be diligently pursued. Those with a talent for the difficult yet noble art of politics,[161] or whose talents in this regard can be developed, should prepare themselves for this role and, forgetting their own convenience and material interests, they should engage in political activity. They must combat injustice and oppression, arbitrary domination and intolerance by individuals or political parties, and they must do so with integrity and wisdom. They must dedicate themselves to the service of all in a spirit of sincerity and fairness, with the charity and the courage demanded by political life.

The Political Community and the Church

76. It is of supreme importance, especially in a pluralistic society, to work out a proper vision of the relationship between the political community and the Church, and to distinguish clearly between what a Christian conscience leads them to do, whether individually or collectively, in their own name as citizens, and their activity in union with their pastors in the name of the Church.

The Church, by reason of her role and competence, is not identified with any political community nor bound by ties to any political system. She is at once the sign and the safeguard of the transcendental dimension of the human person.

The political community and the Church are autonomous and independent of each other in their own fields. Nevertheless, both are devoted to the personal and social vocation of man, though

---

161 Cf. Pius XI, *Allocution to the Directors of the Catholic University Federation: Discorsi di Pio XI*, Vol. 1 (Turin, 1960) , p. 743.

under different titles. This service will redound the more effectively to the welfare of all, insofar as both institutions practice better cooperation according to the local and prevailing situation. For man's horizons are not bounded only by the temporal order; living on the level of human history, he preserves the integrity of his eternal destiny. The Church, for her part, being founded in the love of the redeemer, contributes toward the spread of justice and charity among nations and within the borders of the nations themselves. By preaching the truths of the Gospel and clarifying all sectors of human activity through her teaching and the witness of her members, the Church respects and encourages the political freedom and responsibility of the citizen.

Since the apostles, their successors and all who help them have been given the task of announcing Christ, Savior of the world, to man, they rely in their apostolate on the power of God who often shows forth the force of the Gospel in the weakness of its witnesses. If anyone wishes to devote himself to the ministry of God's Word, let him use the ways and means proper to the Gospel which differ in many respects from those obtaining in the earthly city.

Nevertheless, there are close links between the things of earth and those things in man's condition which transcend the world, and the Church utilizes temporal realities as often as her mission requires it. But she never places her hopes in any privileges accorded to her by civil authority; indeed, she will give up the exercise of certain legitimate rights whenever it becomes clear that their use will compromise the sincerity of her witness, or whenever new circumstances call for a revised approach. But at all times and in all places the Church should have true freedom to preach the faith, to proclaim her teaching about society, to carry out her task among men without hindrance and to pass moral judgments even in matters relating to politics whenever the fundamental rights of man or the salvation of souls requires it. The means, the only means, she may use are those which are in accord with the Gospel and the welfare of all men according to the diversity of times and circumstances.

With loyalty to the Gospel in the fulfillment of her mission in the world, the Church, whose duty it is to foster and elevate all that is true, all that is good and all that is beautiful in the human community,[162] consolidates peace among men for the glory of God.[163]

---

[162] Cf. Vatican Council II, *Dogmatic Constitution on the Church,* n. 13: *A.A.S.* 57 (1965), p. 17.

[163] Cf. Lk. 2, 14.

Study-Club Questions

1. Discuss the nature and purpose of the political community.

2. What are the public duties binding on all citizens?

3. Discuss the right of citizens to defend themselves when they live under an authority that oversteps its competence.

4. What are the responsibilities of governments to minority groups?

5. Why is it now necessary for public authority to intervene more frequently in social, cultural and economic matters?

6. When is it imperative to impose restrictions on the exercise of human rights for the common good? How should this be done?

7. What is the role of the Christian in political life?

8. What is the role of the Church in a pluralistic society?

9. What is the relation of the Church to government? May she ever be bound to one particular political system for any reason?

10. In what way does the Church foster what is true, good and beautiful in the human community?

CHAPTER V

MAINTENANCE OF PEACE AND ESTABLISHMENT OF A COMMUNITY OF NATIONS

Introduction

77. In our generation which has been marked by persistent and acute hardships and anxiety resulting from the ravages of war and the threat of war, the whole human race faces a moment of supreme crisis in its advance toward maturity. Mankind has gradually come closer together and is everywhere more conscious of its own unity, but it wll not succeed in accomplishing the task awaiting it—that is, the establishment of a truly human world for all men over the entire earth—unless everyone devotes himself to the cause of true peace with renewed vigor. Thus the message of the Gospel, which epitomizes the highest ideals and aspirations of mankind, shines anew in our times when it proclaims that the advocates of peace are blessed, "for they shall be called children of God" (Mt. 5, 9).

Accordingly, the Council proposes to outline the true and noble nature of peace, to condemn the savagery of war and to earnestly exhort Christians to cooperate with all in securing a peace based on justice and charity and in promoting the means necessary to attain it under the help of Christ, the author of peace.

Nature of Peace

78.   Peace is more than the absence of war; it cannot be reduced to the maintenance of a balance of power between opposing forces, nor does it arise out of despotic dominion, but it is appropriately called "the work of justice" (Is. 32, 17). It is the fruit of that right ordering of things with which the divine founder has invested human society and which must be actualized by man thirsting after an ever more perfect reign of justice. But while the common good of mankind ultimately derives from the eternal law, it depends in the concrete upon circumstances which change as time goes on; consequently, peace will never be achieved once and for all but must be built up continually. Moreover, since human nature is weak and wounded by sin, the achievement of peace requires both a constant effort to control the passions and unceasing vigilance by lawful authority.

However, this is not enough. Peace cannot be obtained on earth unless the welfare of man is safeguarded and people freely and trustingly share with one another the riches of their minds and their talents. A firm determination to respect the dignity of other men and other peoples as well as the deliberate practice of fraternal love is absolutely necessary for the achievement of peace. Accordingly, peace is also the fruit of love, for love goes beyond what justice can ensure.

Peace on earth, which flows from love of one's neighbor, symbolizes and derives from the peace of Christ who proceeds from God the Father. Christ, the Word made flesh, the Prince of peace, reconciled all men to God by the cross and, restoring the unity of all in one people and one body, he abolished hatred in his own flesh; [164] after being lifted up through his resurrection he poured forth the Spirit of love into the hearts of men. Therefore, all Christians are earnestly to speak the truth in love (cf. Eph. 4, 15) and join with all peace-loving men in pleading for peace and trying to bring it about. In the same spirit we cannot but express our admiration for all who forego the use of violence to vindicate their rights and resort to those means of defense which are also available to weaker parties, provided it can be done without harm to the rights and duties of others and of the community.

Insofar as men are sinners, the threat of war hangs over them and will so continue until the coming of Christ; but insofar as they can vanquish sin by coming together in charity, violence itself will be vanquished and they will make these words come true: ". . . they shall turn their swords into ploughshares, and their spears into sickles. Nation shall not lift up sword against nation, neither shall they be exercised any more to war" (Is. 2, 4).

I

Avoidance of War

Curbing the Savagery of War

79. Even though recent wars have wrought immense material and moral havoc on the world, the devastation of battle still rages in some parts of the world. Indeed, now that every kind of weapon produced by modern science is used in war, the savagery of war threatens to lead the combatants to barbarities far surpassing those of former ages.

---

[164] Cf. Eph. 2, 16; Col. 1, 20-22.

Moreover, the complexity of the modern world and the intricacy of international relations cause wars that have lain dormant to be protracted by new methods of infiltration and subversion. In many cases terrorist methods are regarded as new strategies of war.

Faced by this deplorable state of humanity the Council wishes to remind men that the natural law of peoples and its universal principles still retain their binding force. The conscience of mankind firmly and ever more emphatically proclaims these principles. Any action which deliberately violates these principles and any order which commands such actions is criminal, and blind obedience cannot excuse those who carry them out. The most infamous among these actions are those designed for the reasoned and methodical extermination of an entire race, nation or ethnic minority. These must be condemned as horrendous crimes, and we cannot commend too highly the courage of the men who openly and fearlessly resist those who issue orders of this kind.

On the question of warfare, there are various international conventions, signed by many countries, which seek to render military action and its consequences less inhuman: they deal with the treatment of wounded and interned prisoners of war and with various kindred questions. These agreements must be preserved; indeed, public authorities and specialists in these matters must do all in their power to improve these conventions and thus bring about a better and more effective curbing of the savagery of war. Moreover, it seems just that humane laws should regulate the case of conscientious objectors who refuse to carry arms, provided some other form of community service is substituted.

War, of course, has not ceased to be part of the human scene. As long as the danger of war persists and there is no international authority with the necessary competence and power, governments cannot be denied the right of lawful self-defense, once all peace efforts have failed. State leaders and all who share the burdens of public administration have the duty to defend the interests of their people and to conduct such grave matters with a deep sense of responsibility. However, it is one thing to wage a war of self-defense; it is quite another to seek to impose domination on another nation. The possession of war potential does not justify the use of force for political or military objectives. Nor does the mere fact that war has unfortunately broken out mean that all is fair between the warring parties.

All those who enter the military service in loyalty to their country should look upon themselves as the custodians of the security and freedom of their fellow countrymen; moreover, when they carry out their duty properly, they are contributing to the maintenance of peace.

Total Warfare

80. The development of armaments by modern science has immeasurably magnified the horrors and wickedness of war. Warfare conducted with these weapons can inflict immense and indiscriminate havoc which goes far beyond the bounds of legitimate defense. Indeed, if the kind of weapons now stocked in the arsenals of the great powers were to be employed to the fullest, the result would be the almost complete reciprocal slaughter of one side by the other, not to speak of the widespread devastation that would follow in the world and the deadly aftereffects resulting from the use of such arms.

All these factors force us to undertake a completely fresh reappraisal of war.[165] Men of this generation should realize that they will have to render an account of their warlike behavior; the destiny of generations to come depends largely on the decisions they make today.

With these considerations in mind, the Council, endorsing the condemnations of total warfare issued by recent popes,[166] declares: Every act of war directed to the indiscriminate destruction of whole cities or vast areas with their inhabitants is a crime against God and man which merits firm and unequivocal condemnation.

The hazards peculiar to modern warfare consist in the fact that they expose those possessing recently developed weapons to the risk of perpetrating crimes like these and, by an inexorable chain of events, of urging men to even worse acts of atrocity. To obviate the possibility of this happening at any time in the future, the bishops of the world gathered together implore all men, especially government leaders and military advisors, to give unceasing consideration to their immense responsibilities before God and before the whole human race.

The Arms Race

81.　Undoubtedly, armaments are not amassed

---

[165] Cf. John XXIII, Encyclical Letter *Pacem in terris,* April 11, 1963: *A.A.S.* 55 (1963), p. 291; "Therefore, in this age of ours which prides itself on its atomic power, it is irrational to believe that war is still an apt means of vindicating violated rights."

[166] Cf. Pius XII, Allocution of Sept. 30, 1954: *A.A.S.* 46 (1954), p. 589; Pius XII, Radio Message of Dec. 24, 1954: *A.A.S.* 47 (1955), pp. 15ff.; John XXIII, Encyclical Letter *Pacem in terris: A.A.S.* 55 (1963), pp. 286-91; Paul VI, *Address to the United Nations,* Oct. 4, 1965.

merely for use in wartime. Since the defensive strength of any nation is thought to depend on its capacity of immediate retaliation, the stockpiling of arms which grows from year to year serves, in a way hitherto unthought of, as a deterrrent to potential attackers. Many people look upon this as the most effective way known at the present time for maintaining some sort of peace among nations.

Whatever one may think of this form of deterrent, people are convinced that the arms race, which quite a few countries have entered, is no infallible way for maintaining real peace, and that the resulting so-called balance of power is no sure and genuine path to achieving it. Rather than eliminate the causes of war, the arms race serves only to aggravate the position. As long as extravagant sums of money are poured into the development of new weapons, it is impossible to devote adequate aid to tackling the misery which prevails at the present time in the world. Instead of eradicating international conflict once and for all, the contagion is spreading to other parts of the world. New approaches, based on a renewal of mentality, will have to be chosen in order to remove this stumbling block, to free the earth from its pressing anxieties and to give back to the world a genuine peace.

Therefore, we declare once again that the arms race is one of the greatest curses on the human race, and the harm it inflicts on the poor is more than can be endured. Moreover, there is every reason to fear that if it continues it will bring forth those lethal disasters which are already in preparation. Warned by the possibility of the catastrophes that man has created, let us profit by the respite we now enjoy, thanks to divine favor, to take stock of our responsibilities and find ways of resolving controversies in a manner more worthy of human beings. Providence urgently demands of us that we free ourselves from the age-old slavery of war. If we refuse to make this effort, there is no knowing where we will be led on the fatal path we have taken.

Total Outlawing of War: International Action To Prevent War

82.   It is our clear duty to spare no effort in working for the time when all war will be completely outlawed by international agreement. This goal obviously requires the establishment of a universally acknowledged public authority vested with the effective power to ensure security for all, regard for justice and respect for law. But before this desirable authority can be constituted, it is necessary for existing international bodies to devote themselves resolutely to the exploration of better means for obtaining common security. Since peace must be born of mutual trust between peoples instead of being forced on nations through dread of arms, all must work to put an end to the arms race and make a real beginning of disarmament, not unilaterally indeed but at an equal rate on all sides, on the basis of agreements and supported by genuine and effective guarantees.[167]

In the meantime one must not underestimate the efforts already made or now under way to eliminate the danger of war. On the contrary, support should be given to the goodwill of numerous individuals who are making every effort to eliminate the havoc of war; these men, although burdened by the weighty responsibilities of their high office,

---

[167] Cf. John XXIII, Encyclical Letter *Pacem in terris*, where reduction of arms is mentioned: *A.A.S.* 55 (1963), p. 287.

are motivated by a consciousness of their very grave obligations, even if they cannot ignore the complexity of the situation as it stands. We must beseech the Lord to give them the strength to tackle with perseverance and carry out with courage this task of supreme love for man which is the building up of a lasting peace in a true spirit of manhood. In our times this work demands that they enlarge their thoughts and their spirit beyond the confines of their own country, that they put aside nationalistic selfishness and ambitions to dominate other nations, and that they cultivate deep reverence for the whole of mankind which is painstakingly advancing toward greater maturity.

The problems of peace and disarmament have been treated at length with courage and untiring consultation at negotiations and international meetings; these are to be considered as the first steps toward the solution of such important questions and must be further pursued with even greater insistence, with a view to obtaining concrete results in the future. But people should take care not to entrust these problems to the efforts of a few men, while remaining careless about their own attitudes. For State leaders, who are at once the guardians of their own people and the promoters of the welfare of the whole world, rely to a great extent on public opinion and public attitudes. Their peacemaking efforts will be in vain as long as men are divided and warring among themselves through hostility, contempt and distrust, as well as through racial hatred and uncompromising hostilities. Hence there is a very urgent need of reeducation and renewed orientation of public opinion. Those engaged in the work of education, especially youth education, and the people who mold public opinion should regard it as their most important task to educate the minds of men to renewed sentiments of peace. Every one of us needs a change of heart; we must set our gaze on the whole world and look to those tasks we can all perform together in order to bring about the betterment of our race.

But let us not be buoyed up with false hope. For unless animosity and hatred are put aside and firm, honest agreements about world peace are concluded, humanity may, in spite of the wonders of modern science, go from the grave crisis of the present day to that dismal hour when the only peace it will experience will be the dread peace of death. However, the Church, living in the midst of these anxieties, even as she makes these statements, has not lost hope. She intends to propose to our age over and over again, in season and out of season, the apostle's message: "Behold, now is the acceptable time; behold, now is the day of salvation."[168]

II

ESTABLISHMENT OF AN INTERNATIONAL COMMUNITY

Causes of Discord; Remedies

83.   If peace is to be established the first condition is to root out the causes of discord among men which lead to wars, particularly injustice. Not a few of these causes arise because of excessive economic inequalities and the hesitation to undertake necessary correctives. Some are due to the desire to dominate or contempt for people and, at a deeper level, to envy, distrust, pride and other selfish passions. Man cannot put up with such an

---

[168] Cf. 2 Cor. 6, 2.

amount of disorder; the result is that, even when war is absent, the world is constantly beset by strife and violence between men. Since the same evils are also to be found in relations between nations, it is of the utmost importance, if these evils are to be overcome or forestalled and if headlong violence is to be curbed, for international bodies to work more effectively and more resolutely together and to co-ordinate their efforts; finally, man should work unsparingly toward the creation of organizations designed to promote the cause of peace.

The Community of Nations and International Organizations

84. At the present time when close ties of dependence between individuals and peoples all over the world are developing, the universal common good has to be pursued in an appropriate way and more effectively achieved. Therefore, the community of nations must organize itself in a manner suited to its present responsibilities, with special reference to its obligations to the many areas of the world where intolerable want still prevails. To reach this goal, organizations of the international community, for their part, should seek to provide for the different needs of men; this will involve the sphere of social life, to which belong questions of food, hygiene, education, employment and certain particular situations arising here and there—as, for example, a general need to promote the welfare of developing countries, to alleviate the miseries of refugees dispersed throughout the world and to assist migrants and their families.

Already existing international and regional organizations certainly deserve the enthusiastic support of the human race. They represent the first attempts at laying the foundations on an international level for a community of all men to work toward the solutions of the very serious problems of our times, and specifically toward the encouragement of progress everywhere and the prevention of wars of all kinds. The Church is glad to view the spirit of true brotherhood existing in all spheres between Christians and non-Christians as she seeks to intensify her untiring efforts to alleviate the enormity of human misery.

International Cooperation in Economic Matters

85.   The present solidarity of mankind calls for greater international cooperation in economic matters. Indeed, although nearly all peoples have achieved political independence, they are hardly free from excessive inequalities and every form of undue dependence, and they are far from being immune to serious internal difficulties.

The development of a nation depends on human and financial resources. The citizens of every nation must be prepared to discharge different economic and social functions by education and professional training. This involves the help of experts from abroad who, while they are the bearers of assistance, should not behave as overlords but as helpers and fellow workers. Material aid for developing nations will not be forthcoming unless there is a profound change in the prevailing conventions of commerce today. Other types of aid from affluent nations should take the form of grants, loans or investments; they should be given in a spirit of generosity and without greed on one side, and accepted with complete honesty on the other.

The establishment of an authentic economic order on a worldwide scale can only be effected

through the abolishment of profiteering, nationalistic ambitions, greed for political domination,
militaristic schemes and intrigues aimed at spreading and imposing propaganda and ideology. Different economic and social systems have been
suggested. It is to be hoped that experts will discover in them a common ground for a world commerce based on justice. This will result if all men
abandon their own prejudices and show themselves
ready to enter into sincere discussion.

Some Useful Norms

86. The following norms seem useful for such
cooperation:

a. Developing nations should be firmly convinced that their express and unequivocal aim is
the total human development of their citizens.
They should bear in mind that progress has its
roots and its strength especially in the work and
talent of their citizens. They should also remember
that progress is based not only on foreign aid, but
also on the full utilization of native resources and
on the development of their own culture and traditions. In this matter those who exert the greatest
influence on others should provide outstanding
example.

b. The most important task of the affluent nations is to help developing nations to fulfill these
commitments. Accordingly, they should undertake
within their own confines the spiritual and material adjustments which are needed for the establishment of worldwide cooperation. They should
look to the welfare of the weaker and poorer nations in business dealings with them, since the
revenues the latter make from the sale of home-
produced goods are needed for their own support.

c. It is the responsibility of the international

community to coordinate and stimulate development, but in such a way as to distribute with the maximum fairness and efficiency the resources set aside for this purpose. Its task also includes the organization of economic affairs on a worldwide scale, without transgressing the principle of solidarity, so that business will be conducted according to the norms of justice. Organizations should be established to promote and regulate international commerce, especially with less developed nations, in order to compensate for losses resulting from the excessive inequality of power among the various nations. This kind of organization, accompanied by technical, cultural, and financial aid, should provide nations on the path of progress with all that is necessary for them to achieve adequate economic success.

International Cooperation in Population Expansion Problems

87. International cooperation is vitally necessary in the case of those peoples who very often in the midst of many difficulties are faced with the special problems arising out of rapid increases in population. There is a pressing need to harness the full and eager cooperation of all, particularly of the wealthier nations, in order to explore how the human necessities of food and suitable education can be furnished and shared with the entire human community. Some peoples could improve their standard of living considerably if they were properly trained to substitute new techniques of agricultural production for antiquated methods and adapt them prudently to their own situation. The social order would also be improved and a fairer distribution of land ownership would be assured.

The government assuredly has, in the matter of

the population problem of its country, its own rights and duties within the limits of its proper competence—for instance, as regards social and family legislation, the migration of country dwellers to the city and information concerning the state and needs of the nation. Some men nowadays are gravely disturbed by this problem; it is to be hoped that there will be Catholic experts in these matters, particularly in universities, who will diligently study these problems and pursue their researches further.

Since there is a widespread opinion that the population expansion of the world, or at least of some particular countries, should be kept in check by all possible means and by every kind of intervention by public authority, the Council exhorts all men to beware of all solutions, whether uttered in public or in private or imposed at any time, which transgress the natural law. In virtue of man's inalienable right to marriage and the procreation of children, the decision regarding the number of children depends on the judgment of the parents and is in no way to be left to the decrees of public authority. Now since the parents' judgment presupposes a properly formed conscience, it is of great importance that all should have an opportunity to cultivate a genuinely human sense of responsibility which will take into account the circumstances of time and situation as well as respect the divine law; to attain this goal a change for the better must take place in teaching and social conditions and, above all, religious formation or at least complete moral training must be available. People should be discreetly informed of scientific advances in research into methods of birth regulation whenever the value of these methods has been thoroughly proved and their conformity with the moral order established.

Role of Christians in International Aid

88. Christians should willingly and wholeheartedly support the establishment of an international order that includes a genuine respect for legitimate freedom and friendly sentiments of brotherhood toward all men. It is all the more urgent now that the greater part of the world is in a state of such poverty that it is as if Christ himself were crying out in the mouths of these poor people to the charity of his disciples. Let us not be guilty of the scandal of having some nations, most of whose citizens bear the name of Christians, enjoying an abundance of riches, while others lack the necessities of life and are tortured by hunger, disease and all kinds of misery. For the spirit of poverty and charity is the glory and witness of the Church of Christ.

We must praise and assist those Christians, especially young Christians, who volunteer their services to help men and nations other than their own. Indeed, it is the duty of all Christians, under the teaching and example of the bishops, to do everything in their power to alleviate the hardships of our times, giving generously, as was the ancient custom of the Church, not merely from what is superfluous, but also out of the substance of their goods.

Without organizing methods of collection and distribution in a rigid and uniform way, such ecumenical activity should be properly conducted in dioceses, nations and on a worldwide scale, in collaboration with our other Christian brethren, whenever this seems opportune. Far from being opposed to the careful and ordered exercise of social and charitable action, the spirit of charity demands it. Therefore, it is necessary for those who intend to serve in developing countries to be properly trained in specialized institutes.

Effective Presence of the Church in the International Community

89. The Church, in preaching the Gospel to all men and dispensing the treasures of grace in accordance with her divine mission, makes a contribution to the strengthening of peace over the whole world and helps to consolidate the foundations of brotherly communion among men and peoples. She accomplishes this by imparting the knowledge of the divine and the natural law. Accordingly, to foster and stimulate cooperation among men, the Church must be clearly present in the midst of the community of nations; motivated solely by the desire to be of service to all men, she seeks to achieve her goal both by means of her official channels and through the full and sincere collaboration of all Christians. This goal will be more effectively brought about if all the faithful are conscious of their responsibility as men and as Christians and work in their own environments to arouse generous cooperation with the international community. Special attention should be given in this matter to the training of youth in their religious and civil education.

Role of Christians in International Organizations

90. For Christians, an unquestionably excellent form of international activity is the part they play, either individually or collectively, in organizations already established or to be established which foster

cooperation between nations. Various Catholic international associations can also help the community of nations to achieve peace and brotherhood; these bodies should be strengthened by enlarging the number of well-qualified personnel, by increasing the subsidies they need so badly, and by the suitable coordination of their energies. Nowadays efficiency of action and the need for dialogue call for initiatives in common. Organizations of this kind, moreover, contribute more than a little to the instilling of a feeling of universality, which is certainly appropriate for Catholics, and to the formation of truly worldwide solidarity and responsibility.

Finally, in order that Catholics may properly fulfill their role in the international community, it is hoped that they will seek to cooperate actively and in a positive manner with their separated brethren who are co-sharers with them in professing the charity of the Gospel, as well as with all men who thirst for true peace.

Taking into account the immensity of the hardships which still afflict a large section of humanity, and with a view to fostering everywhere the justice of Christ and his love for the poor, the Council suggests that it would be most opportune to establish an organism of the universal Church whose task would be to arouse the Catholic community to promote the progress of needy regions and to foster social justice between nations.

Study-Club Questions

1. May one ever contravene the natural law on some-one else's orders?

2. Discuss conscientious objection.

3. Why do you think the Constitution declares the arms race to be "one of the greatest curses on the human race"?

4. Because of the weaponry at his disposal, contem-porary man stands on the brink of annihilation. Discuss.

5. Will it ever be possible to heed the call to outlaw war by international agreement? Has it been tried in the past? How successful has it been? What has been overlooked?

6. What are some international organizations now in existence that seek to promote peace and brother-hood throughout the world?

7. What are the responsibilities of the affluent nations to those that are underdeveloped? What are the in-ternal responsibilities of these underdeveloped nations?

8. What are some of the more outstanding difficulties countries are experiencing as a result of rapid population expansion?

9. In the light of the previous question, what steps can be taken to ease the plight of those nations seriously affected by such an expansion?

10. What part should Christians play in international aid and in organizations that foster cooperation between nations?

CONCLUSION

Role of Individual Christians and of Particular Churches

91. Drawn from the treasures of the teaching of the Church, the proposals of this Council are intended for all men, whether they believe in God or whether they do not explicitly acknowledge him; they are intended to help them to a keener awareness of their own destiny, to make the world conform better to the surpassing dignity of man, to strive for a more deeply-rooted sense of universal brotherhood and to meet the pressing appeals of our times with a generous and common effort of love.

Faced with the wide variety of situations and forms of human culture in the world, this conciliar program is deliberately general on many points; indeed, while the teaching presented is one already common in the Church, it will have to be pursued further and amplified because it often deals with matters which are subject to continual development. Nevertheless, we have based our proposals on the Word of God and the spirit of the Gospel. Hence we entertain the hope that many of our suggestions will succeed in effectively assisting many people, especially after they have been adapted to the mentalities of many nations and put into practice by the faithful under the direction of their pastors.

Dialogue between All Men

92. In virtue of her mission to enlighten the whole world with the message of the Gospel and to gather together in one Spirit all men of every nation, race and culture, the Church shows herself as a sign of that spirit of brotherhood by which sincere dialogue is not only made possible but also strengthened.

Such a mission requires us first of all to create in the Church herself mutual esteem, reverence and harmony and to acknowledge all legitimate diversity; in this way all who constitute the one People of God will be able to engage in ever more fruitful dialogue, whether they are pastors or ordinary members of the faithful. For the ties which unite the faithful together are stronger than those which separate them; let there be unity in what is necessary, freedom in what is doubtful, and charity in everything.[169]

At the same time our thoughts go out to those brothers and communities not yet living in full communion with us; yet we are united by our worship of the Father, the Son and the Holy Spirit and by bonds of love. We are also mindful that the unity of Christians is today awaited and longed for by many non-believers. For the more this unity is realized in truth and charity under the powerful impulse of the Holy Spirit, the more it will be a harbinger of unity and peace throughout the whole world. Let us then join our forces and modify our methods in a way that is suitable and effective today for achieving this lofty goal, and let us pattern ourselves daily more and more after the spirit of the Gospel and work together in a spirit of brotherhood to serve the human family which has been

---

169 Cf. John XXIII, Encyclical Letter *Ad Petri cathedram*, June 29, 1959: *A.A.S.* 55 (1959), p. 513.

called to become in Christ Jesus the family of the sons of God.

Our thoughts also go out to all who acknowledge God and who preserve precious religious and human elements in their traditions; it is our hope that frank dialogue will spur us all on to receive impulses of the Spirit with fidelity and to act upon them with alacrity.

For our part, our eagerness for such dialogue, conducted with appropriate discretion and leading to truth by way of love alone, excludes no one; we would like to include those who respect outstanding human values without realizing who the author of those values is, as well as those who oppose the Church and persecute her in various ways. Since God the Father is the beginning and the end of all things, we are all called to be brothers; therefore, we must work together without violence and without deceit to build up the world in a spirit of genuine peace.

A World To Be Built Up and Brought to Fulfillment

93. Mindful of the words of the Lord: "By this will all men know that you are my disciples, if you have love for one another" (Jn. 13, 35), Christians can yearn for nothing more ardently than to serve the men of this age with an ever growing generosity and success. Holding loyally to the Gospel, enriched by its resources and joining forces with all who love and practice justice, they have shouldered a weighty task here on earth and they must render an account of it to him who will judge all men on the last day. Not everyone who says "Lord, Lord" will enter the kingdom of heaven, but those who do

the will of the Father [170] and who manfully put their hands to the work. It is the Father's will that we should recognize Christ our brother in the persons of all men and love them with an effective love, in word and in deed, thus bearing witness to the truth; it is also his will that we should share with others the mystery of his heavenly love. In this way men all over the world will awaken to a lively hope (the gift of the Holy Spirit) that they will one day be admitted to the haven of surpassing peace and happiness in their homeland radiant with the glory of the Lord.

"Now, to him who is able to accomplish all things in a measure far beyond what we ask or conceive, in keeping with the power that is at work in us—to him be glory in the Church and in Christ Jesus down through all the ages of time without end. Amen" (Eph. 3, 20-21).

* * *

Each and every point stated in this Constitution has satisfied the fathers of the sacred Council. And we, by the authority bestowed on us by Christ, together with the venerable fathers, approve it in the Holy Spirit, we decree it and we enact it; and we order the promulgation, to God's glory, of what has been enacted synodically.

Rome, in St. Peter's Basilica, December 7, 1965
Paul, Bishop of the Catholic Church

(The fathers' signatures follow)

---

[170] Cf. Mt. 7, 21.